To Stve

Think Smart - Live Rich!

Wishing
you all
the best in
the world

S. Gilbert
Oct
2015

Simon J Gilbert

Visit Simon's website at www.simonjgilbert.com

Email: simon@simonjgilbert.com

Copies are available at special prices for bulk orders

Front cover designed by MM Productions

The publication is designed to provide accurate and authoritative information in regard to the subject matter covered. It is sold with the understanding that the publisher is not engaged in rendering legal, accounting or other professional services. If legal advice or expert assistance is required in this area, the services of a competent professional should be sought.

First published in the UK by Mackenzie Books in 2015

Author's note: Many of the names and identifying circumstances of the people in this book have been changed to protect the individuals privacy.

For Eliza, my beautiful, feisty little girl.....

Contents

Introduction

"There is little success where there is little laughter."
— Andrew Carnegie

Can I be up front and straight with you right from the start? This book is not about the airy-fairy world of "I wish" or "I hope." This book is a practical guide to sorting your head out once and for all. It's about understanding why you get the results you do and learning how to change your results-fast. Learning how to apply the laws of your mind to the direction you want to go in life is one of the most important and valuable things you can ever discover.

After many, many years I've come to realise that what most people want in life is to simply feel really good about themselves. People don't really want the mansions, the cars and the holidays, what they *really* want is how these things will make them feel when they get them. Paradoxically, in the process of discovering and developing the true riches within you'll start to feel totally differently about yourself, and in doing so, you'll begin to attract a much more prosperous and abundant lifestyle regardless. How we feel and what we experience has absolutely nothing to do with anybody or anything external to us, it's always an inside job.

Most of us have an awful lot of undeveloped skills and talents just lying dormant waiting for someone or something else to awaken them and set them free. The biggest challenge for most of us is that we don't see ourselves as we could be, only as we have been in the past. We then keep on repeating behaviours that don't work.

That's pretty dumb when you really stop and think about it. When you know who you really are, and what you've got going for you, you stand a much better chance of getting what you want. You start to believe in yourself so much that it's only a matter of time before you pull off something really big. Throughout this book I intend to change your perception of you so much that you will find it virtually impossible to return to your old ways of thinking about yourself in the same way.

The system you are about to learn contains a unique bringing together of ideas, methods and techniques that can rapidly convert mediocrity, boredom and frustration into power, energy and excitement. Some of the individual aspects of this system are well trodden, some of them you will have never seen or read before. They have all, however, been practiced, tested and proven by thousands of men and women before you, to guarantee the fastest return of your time invested.

By living daily with these concepts and ideas, you will experience a much higher level of control, purpose and self-direction. You will discover and uncover the true cause of your results up until this point. More importantly you will learn how to change them to suit whatever lifestyle you choose. You can have the things you want-all of them, and you will have them when you start to understand who you really are and just how powerful your mind is.

The entrepreneur in me detests conformity and mediocrity.

Just because most people agree that you should do something is probably a good indicator that you shouldn't! If you look around you'll see that most people are wrong about most things. When most people are buying, the clever are selling. When most people are getting into a market the smart are getting out. Most people don't learn anything about themselves and that's why they stay stuck. I know you don't want to be like *most* people, because if you did, you wouldn't be reading a book like this!

This book is about thinking for yourself.

When I was kid, I didn't think for myself. I was totally out of control and totally in conformity to other peoples ways of "how things should be done." I had very little confidence in myself, I knew absolutely nothing about myself and had no idea where I was going. Ultimately, I used to allow others to do the choosing for me. After all, what the hell did I know, I was just a daft young kid, trying to get by, trying not to make too many *wrong* choices. That was pretty much my game, doing ok so long as I didn't rock the boat too much. Have you ever felt like that? I think most people have........

In March of 1988, if you'd have been with me, you would have seen a naïve, 17 year old apprentice mechanic serving petrol in a small village garage. Grateful for the YTS or Youth Training Scheme of the day, I was *choosing* to work fifty hours a week for just £28.50. My total possessions at that time consisted of a red Yamaha 50cc moped, a Smokey and the Bandit video (in Betamax format of course!) and a signed polaroid photo of me and Kevin Keegan........

Every morning, when I arrived at the garage my first job would be to shovel up the dog turds left overnight from Snowy the resident guard dog. Snowy was an aggressive, not-to-be-trusted German Shepherd whose main purpose in life was to prevent people breaking in and stealing stuff. Every day I would get down on my hands and knees and scrub away the result of Snowy's overnight patrolling-only to find myself rolling around in it later, when attempting to fix a customer's car....

In the wintertime, I would have to get reacquainted with "Betty." Betty was a very old, waste-oil heater and needed cleaning out every morning, just to get the garage temperature up above freezing. This was a horrible job and would constantly leave me with dirty black, cracked skin and fingernails. You were allowed to wear latex gloves to clean Betty, but you were branded a tart if you did!

As a result of working in a garage, I was often embarrassed at the state of my hands and would try to hide them away from the people I cared about. At the time, I have to admit, I was really concerned about what other people thought of me.

Through time, I moved up through the ranks and finally qualified as a motor mechanic. I left Snowy and Betty behind to work at larger and cleaner garages, but it was never really what I wanted to do. A big part of my problem was the non-stop little voice inside my head that kept telling me, "THERE'S NOTHING BETTER OUT THERE FOR YOU, JUST BE GRATEFUL FOR WHAT YOU'VE GOT, YOU'RE NOT GOOD ENOUGH TO DO SOMETHING ELSE." You know the voice right? The same voice that keeps reminding you, "WHO DO YOU THINK YOU ARE?" or "WHO THE HELL NEEDS YOU?"

When I was younger I was always run by fear, so it wasn't surprising that I held on to what little I had, never really believing in myself and going after what I *really* wanted. Over the years I turned down a lot of potentially great jobs. On one occasion I turned down an opportunity from a friend to work on the oil rigs in the North Sea. It sounded great *and* paid four times as much money-I just didn't have the balls to take a chance. Fear had won again.

Over the years people could obviously see something in me that I just could not see in myself. I always got on with people easily, got offered a lot of opportunities and I guess that's why I was so frustrated. Something was telling me inside I could achieve a lot more, but at the same time something was holding me back. Sound familiar?

When I was twenty-eight I found myself working as a manager in a small garage. Every week, Mike the local tool-sales rep would visit us once a week in his big Mercedes truck.

One day I was in the process of helping one of the mechanics remove a gearbox out of a customer's car, when I heard Mike roll up in his truck. The car was high up on the lift and as Dave the mechanic undid the last bolt holding it in, the gearbox came out quicker than anyone expected. To prevent it from smashing on the floor I supported it as best I could on one knee, at the same time allowing transmission fluid to run all down my trousers and all over my boots.

As Mike walked towards me I stared right at him whilst surrounded in this pool of filthy gearbox oil. Every week he would turn up all clean and smiling with a pocket full of cash and this week was no different. As I looked at him, then back at me covered in oil, I made an instant decision-I was finally getting out of here no matter what! It felt like the universe was continually sending me messages that there was something better but I just kept ignoring them-mainly because of fear. This time the pain was sufficient to make the decision to change things once and for all.

After three months of scanning all available business opportunities and going through the application process, I ironically bought the same tool franchise as Mike, had *my own* brand new Mercedes van and was allocated the Middlesbrough and Redcar territory as my patch. Not only that but I'd also unknowingly acquired the UK's number one sales manager as my trainer and mentor into the bargain.

This was a definite turning point in my life. Getting a coach or mentor is one of the best things you can possibly do. Having someone in your corner supporting you is vital. In fact, I can't think of anyone who has achieved anything of substance without getting help from other people. Have you got someone like that?

I was getting trained weekly, by the best in the business and was surrounded by winners. With my mentors help and in my very first year I sold more tools than any other trainee, and was named 1998 "Rookie" of the year for the entire UK. I wasn't special, all I did was what I was told to do-and got on with it.

Over the next few years I devoured more and more sales and personal development material from lots of different trainers and teachers and I began teaching what I learnt to anyone who would listen. I was like a sponge soaking up anything that could help me and others improve. I became fascinated with all aspects of sales and behavioural psychology and ultimately managed to grow the sales of that tool business over 500% percent within three years, before cashing out.

With the proceeds I travelled all round New Zealand for a few months before becoming restless and finally decided to move back to the UK. This time I wanted to test myself with a proper start up business rather than a franchise, so I started a unique cleaning business. After three hard months though it wasn't really making any money. I was great at selling, but I hadn't learnt a damn thing about marketing. I didn't know how to attract good customers in the first place. Once again, I hit the books, courses and seminars and very quickly implemented what the experts said to do. The first week I tried a free marketing strategy it generated over £1600 in just one week, where previously I was struggling to make £400.

A success pattern was starting to emerge although I didn't know it at the time. In everything that I did in sport, business or life, mindset was THE most important aspect of all. Psychology always precedes sales and marketing success.

I've discovered that we will only implement new strategies to the degree that our current mindset allows. If a new idea is a lot bigger than your current results in that area, the mind usually rejects this new idea as impossible, unlikely or not viable.

As I continued to read books attend courses and implement everything I learned, I quickly discovered I loved teaching and learning just as much as the actual implementation. All in all I've probably put in more than fifteen thousand hours of study. All of it had one thing in common. Practical understanding of what works and what doesn't, taught by experts from all over the world who have been there before me. I've done exactly the same with learning mindset as I did with sales and marketing.

I've flown all over the planet, invested tens of thousands of pounds of my own money and listened to some of the greatest teachers in history explain exactly how our minds work. I've devoured hours upon hours of audio programs, read hundreds of huge volumes on behavioural psychology, studied the latest cutting edge neuroscience advancements in long weekend seminars and mastermind groups all with just one single purpose;

How do we *really* use our minds to get all the things we say we want-faster? How do we get the real riches of life?

Let it be known right at the outset that when I'm talking of riches, I have in mind *all* riches-not merely those represented by private jets, oceanfront properties and large bank accounts. However if you really want these things - then good on you! You don't have to justify your chosen lifestyle to me or anyone else for that matter. I'm talking about the real riches of doing *what* you want, *when* you want with *whom* you want. To buy into anything other than how you really want to live is to buy into a story of scarcity and limitation.

Over the years there's a book that's become very dear to my heart-Napoleon Hill's "Think And Grow Rich." It's a real ground breaker in the field mainly because Hill spent more than 20 years doing an awful lot of the grunt work that provides the basis of a lot of present day material. Hill studied over 500 of the world's most successful self-made business people and 16,000 so called "failures" way back in the early 1900's. Hill's purpose was to fast-track the average guys journey from poverty to riches in such a way that was clear, definitive and guaranteed.

Having run many Mastermind groups over the last ten years with hundreds of participants and consulted with many private clients in business, it's become clear to me that there are really only four key elements needed in order to live a really rich life and start winning. They are,

1. Desire-generated by the clarity of what you want.

2. The belief that you will get it.

3. A plan to put that belief into action.

4. Persistence.

You have to really, really want something, have an idea as to how to get it, totally believe it and keep going. What I have found over the years though, is that if you manage to get the desire and the clarity part sorted out, most people still don't believe in themselves *enough* to live their personal path to riches.

Hill makes it perfectly clear that his system will work for anybody who chooses to adopt it - the problem is most people don't. So why not? Why don't people act on the very information that could transform their lives for the better and turn worry and frustration into confidence and action? After all my intensive research and practical experience in this area, I believe the biggest problem people face on a daily basis is simply........... FEAR.

Fear is the biggest problem in your life today.

It's a bit of a bold statement considering I don't really know you yet, but let me tell you why. Studies show that *most* people never get to the end of *most* books. In fact the majority of people start reading the first chapter with good intention, only to find something else grab their attention before they finish it.

Hill unfortunately leaves one of the most important chapters of his entire philosophy, right until the end. In the chapter, "How to Outwit the Six Ghosts of Fear", he lays things out for us quite simply;

"BEFORE you can put ANY portion of the Think and Grow Rich philosophy into successful use, your mind must be **prepared to receive it.** The preparation is not that difficult. It begins with study, analysis and an understanding of three enemies which you shall have to clear out."

"These enemies are INDECISION, DOUBT and FEAR!"

If it is true that all thoughts eventually manifest themselves into their physical equivalent, it must be equally true that thoughts of fear CANNOT be translated into actions of belief and confidence.

Hill knew that fear was the killer of ambition and the champion of mediocrity. He knew that understanding fear was necessary for those who would accumulate riches. He knew that fear was hidden in the subconscious mind, but what he didn't know, at that time, was how to identify and eliminate the fear that paralyses so many people in business.

The knowledge just wasn't available back then.

It is my intention in this book to explain why fear shows up for us so often and what it *really* is, so you can start to release its unconscious grip on your mind. More importantly though, you'll learn how to identify and eliminate any belief that's holding you back from everything you've ever wanted.

I'm actually going to teach you the exact same system I use with my private clients so you can start to eliminate the beliefs, thoughts and fears sabotaging your success in business. I'm going to lay it all out for you, step by step with nothing held back. In just a couple of hours reading you will finally understand how to finally eliminate fear, get unstoppable confidence and live a rich life of your own personal choosing. Are you ready to give fear one final kick in the nuts? Great! Let's go then......

Chapter 1

Screw Fear!

S ome people always do well, no matter what is happening around them. They make fabulous money, live in nice homes, drive new cars and are continually taking trips abroad. They always seem to have cash on the hip.

Best of all, they are happy, optimistic, positive, friendly, relaxed and always seem to be in complete control of their lives. They are the top performers in any organisation and their skills and attitudes always get the job done.

Over the years thousands of hours and millions of pounds has been spent studying the most successful people in our country. These people have been analysed, shadowed and interviewed. As a result of all this information that is available today, we now know more about what it takes for you to be your best self than we have ever known before. And the most important thing we have learned from all this information is that success is more *psychological* than anything else.

Quite a while ago I was delivering a seminar on mind-power to a group of entrepreneurs, network marketers and sales people. I asked the audience to write down all the things they thought were sabotaging their efforts. All the things they *know* they should be doing, but weren't, down on paper. Just for fun I remarked it shouldn't be a very long list, for all they needed to do was just write a big **ME** at the top of the page! I can confidently say that by reading and implementing the strategies in this book you are literally standing on a major breakthrough in your productivity, freedom and confidence. All by-products of creating the income you want to choose for yourself.

Just by discovering what is at the very core, the *real cause* of your results in business or in life, you can, if you choose to, make a huge shift in your results and start thinking much bigger automatically.

I know this because I've seen it happen for myself and for the hundreds of clients I've sat down with and worked out what the *real* obstacles are that are sabotaging their desired lifestyle. Success *always* follows thinking. And whatever you think about *you* is the most important thing of all.

> *"The truth is not for all men, but only for those who seek it"*
> *- Ayn Rand*

The Big Guns

Two men attend a success seminar. The first guy uses what he has learnt to achieve his goals; the second does not. Instead, the second guy allows fear, lack of clarity, procrastination and self-sabotage to destroy his efforts-never accomplishing the very thing he says he wants. Yes, despite walking over hot coals, breaking arrows with his Adams apple and high-fiving some fat bloke from Hull he quickly realises nothing has *really* changed and soon comes crashing down off his 'motivational' weekend.

This dilemma-and my own personal experience with lack of implementation in business, has led me on a relentless, near 30 year journey of what *really* keeps people from standing out and doing the very things they say they are going to do.

Many people in the training and development industry have spoken out loud about their disappointment and frustration in the lack of actual *implementation* of the information available to us. Information that if implemented, would definitely increase our sales, make us more money and make us more productive.

As illustrated in Figure 1, studies have shown that 80% of people who go on a seminar, read a book, or listen to audio program never do a damn thing with the information they see or hear. Only 15% give it a go, and only 5%, yes just 5% actually *implement* the new information and get a result. It's these people that get outstanding returns on their investment and go on to ever increasing levels of success.

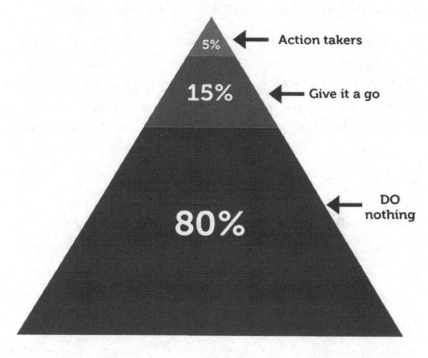

Figure 1

These figures of course fit beautifully with the 80/20 rule or the so called "Pareto Principle."

They also demonstrate that there is something much bigger and illusive going on that surely demands an answer, and that these figures haven't changed one bit, even with the vast amount of information available to us today via the internet. Clearly, the answer does not lie in gathering more information, it is to be found in the mind-set of the individual who takes action on it. In some large companies it is common for some salespeople to be earning £35,000 a year, whilst others with the same product, selling at the same price, into the same market are making £35,000 a month!

Is it possible that the higher earners are twelve times better in any area than the person earning one twelfth as much? No, of course not. In fact sometimes the person earning the big money is younger, works fewer hours and has less experience than some of the older more experienced salespeople who are barely making a living.

This book is going to show you why some people move ahead with ease and others struggle all there life, not knowing they could have changed their results anytime they choose. This requires, more than anything, clearing out your head of all the rubbish that's been dumped in there. All your limiting beliefs, fears and doubts you've picked up over the years so you can develop the top performers mind-set and finally get the rewards you deserve.

You may have heard that promise before, maybe hundreds of times. But I guarantee you this: If you fully understand the processes within this book *and* implement them, life will NEVER be the same again for you.

Make FEAR Your Bitch!

Whatever you design in your life will either shrink or expand directly in proportion to the courage you have to pursue what you really want. Everything lies on the other side of fear the old saying goes, or at least, the illusion of fear. In order to move ahead rapidly in business you must eliminate the three biggest fears that cripple achievement – fears that actually rank above death for some people. They are,

#1 the fear of REJECTION

#2 the fear of FAILURE, and

#3 the fear of CRITICISM

Notice the KEY word I use here. <u>ELIMINATE</u>. Not overcome. Not conquer. Not get over. Telling people to *"Feel the fear and do it anyway"* is an ineffective, outdated and limited strategy for success. If you doubt this just refer back to the "Triangle of Truth" on page 19!

If 95 percent of people aren't feeling it and aren't doing it then obviously we have a much bigger problem on our hands than we think. Inspirational quotes just aren't cutting it. In order to get cast iron results that really work for you permanently, you have to get a much deeper understanding of the *cause* of fear. You have to ditch all the nice, warm and fuzzy success quotes, (that do little more than perpetuate disempowerment) and get a proper understanding of what you're really up against. You have to **THINK SMART** and **LIVE RICH**!

Let's take an example. In network marketing a new distributor may get people excited, show them all these amazing stories of success, a compensation plan that pays well, products or services that work wonders, and a leadership team with a strong track record. They say YES to the opportunity! And they are well excited. They are going to be RICH! They are going to CHANGE THE WORLD and create financial and personal freedom for themselves.

But then they suddenly quit-WHY?

Well, the main reason is that every decision a person makes – EVERY DECISION – is driven by just 2 things:

1. To avoid pain.

2. To gain pleasure.

So, they do "see it." They do see the possibilities. They see the success. They see a need for the product or service in the world. They believe in the people in the up-line....but they never really get the success they want. Why?

Because unfortunately, of the two forces that drive people – AVOIDING PAIN is far more powerful than gaining pleasure.

So, you get the newbie enrolled, order their kit, schedule their first event. They are excited. Full of hope. They are sending you texts, calling you...all is going great.

Then something happens. They start avoiding your calls. They cancel their first meeting. They say "Nobody can make it." "Everyone is busy." What happened?

Here's what happened: They started calling, all excited about their new business opportunity and they get their first, "NO!" Ouch! That hurts. REJECTION kicks in, it feels like FAILURE and to boot one of their friends mocked them for getting into one of those "daft" pyramid things. Bosh! The fear of CRITICISM gets a grip and they get a sharp three way hit of fear all in one blow.

There is no way they are going to keep calling. Hell no. This is PAIN. People don't like pain. And the pain of rejection, failure and criticism seem far bigger (and more real) in the moment, than the *potential* pleasure of earning an extra £500, £1,000 and so on. The mind says, "If THIS is what it takes to make £10,000 a month, I'm outta here!"

How about if you're an Entrepreneur and were looking for potential funding from an investor? Maybe you fancied your chances on TV's Dragons Den? You'd probably have a certain level of anxiety about getting grilled on your business I'm sure. But why? The same three culprits are back again.... rejection, failure and criticism.

What about if you're a salesperson and you have to visit a potential new area with a new product or you're a seasoned salesperson and you have to call on *that* door....yes, that door that you drive past every day and don't call on because you've convinced yourself that they probably won't be interested, or they'll be too busy or......just fill in the blank.

So, how do you develop the Rhino skin, charge down all opposition and bulldoze your way to success like a lot of other books tell you to do?......err, actually ....you <u>don't</u>.

You don't need thicker skin, what you really need is the internal understanding and awareness of what is controlling how and why you feel like this in the first place. Awareness is the greatest secret of all time.

Come with me now as we blow the lid off the world of personal development fact and fiction. It's time that someone told you the truth about what really works and what doesn't, so you can actually start implementing all you've learned over the years and get the results you want. So, first up, we need to lay down the foundations and get a real understanding of these truths before we finally begin to **THINK SMART and LIVE RICH!**

> *"The cave you fear to enter holds the treasure you seek*
> *– Joseph Campbell*

TRUTH #1 – Fear is the Dominant Problem in Your Life Today

Fear is, and always has been, one of the greatest enemies of the entrepreneur and salesperson. It is the greatest obstacle to success in your life and your career. It is both subtle and devastating. It works on you deep inside your subconscious mind, and causes you to see the world negatively instead of with hope and positivity. It causes you to associate with other people who think, feel and believe the same way. You literally reinforce each other's fears and beliefs.

This cumulative effect on your personality can be deadly. As you know, who you surround yourself with is vitally important. For you to achieve great success in sales, (or business in general) the eradication of fear as an influence in your life is job Numero Uno.

The three big fears of rejection, failure and criticism are the biggest problem in the world of the entrepreneur, salesperson or network marketer. They do more damage combined to paralyse your thinking, kill self-reliance, undermine enthusiasm, and encourage and promote procrastination, than ANYTHING else. They destroy ambition, promote indecision and can leave you with total unhappiness.

Because the majority of people suffer from one or all three of these fears, we just accept them as part of what you have to go through to be successful. "You've got to get out of your comfort zone!" the lemmings scream, but this is obviously one of the biggest and most widely held misconceptions of all time. Here's why;

Most psychologists agree that we are only born with just three fears:

- The fear of falling.

- The fear of loud noises, and

- The fear of being abandoned.

These inborn fears *were* given to you to help you monitor what goes on around you. Think about it: It is fear that gives you an adrenaline rush so that you'll have the ability to flee from a situation that is truly unsafe, or the same adrenaline rush to fight to survive. So yes, *these* fears were instilled in you over countless generations as a means of protection and to keep you safe, but these were the *only* fears that were. Burn this following statement right into your mind.

The fears of Rejection, Failure and Criticism that you have now, you have **learnt**. You weren't born with them. Nobody is.

Really stop and think about this statement. This is fantastic news for us because what it means is this,

If you have learnt fear, you can also……unlearn it.

Have you ever seen a self-conscious baby? No, of course not. Why? Because the baby hasn't *learnt* how to be self-conscious. It took countless repetitions of observing it's environment before it knew how to "do" self-conscious. You've never seen a baby that was concerned about what other people thought of him or her have you? Again, it had to be learnt. Fear of rejection, failure and criticism, are *learnt* processes. It's the awareness of these facts that's necessary to help you move ahead and start winning.

If you've done a lot of personal growth you'll know there is a well-known and simple strategy for success. "Success leaves clues." In other words, find out what other successful people have done in that area and model them. Maybe take them out to lunch or give them a call and ask them what they do and how they do it. Pretty good advice right? But how many people actually do it? Hardly any. If you asked the people who know this strategy why they don't use it, they would probably tell you *"Oh you know, I don't want to bother people or they'll probably be too busy."* But again, that's just bollocks. The real cause is the fear of rejection, the fear of failure and the fear of criticism.

The Imposter Syndrome

Amongst high achievers there is another real dilemma called "Imposter Syndrome." If you've ever thought to yourself, "One of these days people will realise I don't know as much as they think", then you are in excellent company!

Many successful people have the little devil sitting on their shoulder whispering, "What are you doing here? What do you think you're doing? You're going to get found out!" Academy Award winning actress Kate Winslet confided in a magazine interview: "I often wake up in the morning before going off to a shoot and think, I can't do this; I'm a fraud."

Needless to say, the list of people who sometimes worry about being uncovered as an impostor is as impressive as it is long. Having to live with a nagging fear of being "found out", as not being as *smart or talented or good enough (or whatever)* as people think, is a common phenomenon.

So common in fact, that the term "Impostor Syndrome" was coined to describe it way back in the 1980's. Indeed, top psychologists and researchers believe that as many as 96% of successful people have suffered from it at some point.

What really matters most though is not whether we occasionally (or regularly) fear failing, look foolish or don't feel good enough, it's whether we give these fears the power to keep us from taking the actions needed to achieve our goals and our highest aspirations. Unfortunately, too often we do just that.

Imposter syndrome is the domain of the top performer. Those who set the bar lower than a rattlesnakes belly are rarely it's victim. So how do you overcome it? That's right. You don't. You permanently eliminate it and shift it for good.

If you are relating to what I'm sharing, then pat yourself on the back, because it's a sure sign that you aren't ready to settle into the comfortable DFS sofa of sameness and mediocrity. Rather, you're likely to be a person who really does wants to succeed and is committed to giving your very best to whatever endeavour you set your sights upon. Think about this. If you permanently eliminated all the beliefs and fears stopping you from taking the necessary actions, what do you think you would be capable of achieving?

The reality is that many, many people are stretching and struggling day in-day out. Perhaps not in exactly the same way, but in their own way, with their own unique set of challenges, insecurities and internal struggles.

Too often we fall into the trap of comparing our *insides* with others *outsides*; our weaknesses with others strengths. We mentally say to ourselves, "If only I could speak with the confidence and humour of Steve, if only I could win the business as fast as Claire." or "If only I was as productive as Simon." Meanwhile, all the Steve's and Claire's and Simon's are thinking: "If only I was as good with people, or leading teams, or creating strategy as you....

Fear of being "found out" can sabotage success on multiple fronts as it drives us to settle for less than what we want and steers us a wide berth from situations that might expose our "perceived" inadequacy and unworthiness. Yet, while our fears urge to us to stick with what we know we're good at – where risk of being uncovered is minimised, letting fear sit at the captain's table is a sure fire recipe for a life of lacklustre mediocrity and frustration.

"The Imposter Syndrome" is again underpinned and directly related to the fears of rejection, failure and criticism.

Fear of Speaking Up

I was recently speaking to a group of young business owners at Leeds University. The speaker on before me was asked a question by a member of the audience about how to conquer (there's that word again, implying it's something to get over) the fear of public speaking. The answer the speaker gave was a very common one based on the understanding most people have about this fear. Her answer? "Just keep doing it, it's the only way!" "*Feel the fear!*", is the rallying cry. Everyone in the room nods in agreement......

According to the National Institute of Mental Health, 74 percent of people have various levels of anxiety when speaking in either a group or public setting. Yet, as I mentioned before, the psychologists tell us the *only* fears we are born with genetically are falling, loud noises and abandonment-all for our protection. So what's going on? What's the *real* cause of the many fears we experience today in business? What really causes the fear of speaking in public, the "Imposter Syndrome" and the fear of rejection, failure and criticism so prevalent in our society today?

Truth #2 – Fear is a Liar!

What made fear (which was supposed to be for our protection) turn into the number one problem in business or life today? Why do people let this crippling mental disease control their feelings, actions, results and ultimately their lives?

The reason is simply this:

People have never stopped and made the distinction between fear and what *causes* the fear in the first place.

Fear is an effect. The *cause* of fear is limiting beliefs, conditioned responses, and interpretations of specific events that you are making in your mind-moment to moment.

Most people react to their fear by avoiding it, ignoring it, or denying it. They let it continually sabotage their efforts or even worse let it permanently interfere with their dreams and ambitions.....because at some level they *think* the fear is real....

If most people have developed limiting beliefs in their early years that *causes* the fear of rejection, most people WILL fear rejection—not because they were born with the fear, but because they have grown specific beliefs during their early years that really does cause the problem!

How can I be so sure that beliefs, interpretations and conditioned responses are responsible for the fear of rejection or most other fears prevalent in business today?

Because hundreds of people who had these fears eliminated the fear permanently when they eliminated certain limiting beliefs and conditioned responses. They never had to *"feel the fear and do it anyway"* anymore. The negative emotions that had been sabotaging their success had vanished. The fear was gone.

Truth #3 – Fear is Crippling

Fearing rejection can lead people to being afraid to take chances and do things they would not ordinarily do, in order to get the approval of others. They generally worry about rejection from others before they do anything. It is not a pleasant way to live.

Getting rid of a few specific beliefs will convince you that your real human nature is to act *without* concern for the opinion of others and without the fears of rejection, failure or criticism.

"It is impossible to live without failing at something, unless you live so cautiously that you might as well never have lived at all."
– J. K. Rowling

Richard Branson quite rightly states that the fear of failure is the major reason as to why most entrepreneurs never start or stop well short of incredible levels of success and achievement. We are afraid to make mistakes and fail too often. The trouble with this is that anytime you are trying something new, something that hasn't been proven to work before, there is always the possibility of making a mistake or failure.

Most business coaches would encourage people to *overcome* this fear and give them tips on how to do it, but it still doesn't go away. I totally agree with Branson in that what is needed most in this world is innovation that is turned into products and services to be sold. I also agree that fear of making mistakes and failing is one of the biggest barriers preventing people from actually doing this.

Yes, we do have a reptilian brain where the only thing that counts is our survival. That's why anything we perceive as threatening to our survival will produce the emotion of fear. But what determines what we perceive to be a threat to our survival? You won't be surprised when I say the answer is beliefs - in this case though, two very specific beliefs.

Truth #4 – Where Limiting Beliefs Really Come From

What makes people fear "mistakes and failure" are two beliefs that most people seem to have: "Mistakes and failure are bad," and "If I make a mistake or fail, I'll be rejected." If you believe it is bad to make a mistake or fail and that you will be rejected if you do either of these two things, you *will* experience fear, and in most cases the fear will prevent or inhibit action dramatically.

So, why are these two beliefs so common? Well, let's take a look at how they were formed. Most parents never take parenting classes on learning how to be an effective parent and most parents bring their own "beliefs" with them to the job of parenting. Moreover, most parents have unreasonable expectations for their children. For example, most parents expect little kids to come when called, sit still, not make too much noise, and do what they are told to do. All of these things are virtually impossible for a little kid. As a parent of two small children I know first-hand that kids want to do what *they* want to do, when they want to do it, irrespective of what I might want!

How do parents usually respond when their expectations are not met? In the best of cases, they respond with mild annoyance and frustration, but in the worst of cases, with physical abuse. The reaction of most parents is somewhere in between these two extremes. Most parents get angry and repeat the phrases that have become clichés in our society: "How many times do I have to tell you?" "Don't you ever listen?" "Why can't you do what I tell you?" "What's wrong with you?" Many of my clients tell me about their parents "look."

What meaning or interpretation does a 3 to 6-year-old child give to his parents response? "I'm not doing what my parents want. I don't seem to be able to give them what they want. I'm making mistakes and failing. Mam and Dad are angry, that must be bad. Because it feels like my parents don't love me when they are angry at me and it feels like they are withdrawing from me, it feels like I'm being rejected."

This is not to put the blame on the parents for the beliefs you now hold. At the time they were only working with a very limited amount of knowledge, experience and awareness of how a small child could interpret their actions and behaviours. Later on you are going to find out that although you were small you still chose your beliefs (no pity parties on my watch!).

Most schools also create an environment in which these two beliefs are likely to be formed as well. However, most kids have *already* started to create these beliefs at home *before* they ever get to school.

How do I know this? Because my associates and I have helped hundreds of clients permanently eliminate the beliefs that *cause* the fears of rejection, failure, criticism, self-sabotage, public speaking, procrastination, and a whole bunch of other limiting patterns of unwanted behaviours in business as well. My findings agree with what psychologists have been saying for years; beliefs are formed early. Eliminate the beliefs that support and hold fear in place, and fear will be eliminated permanently. More importantly, behaviour *will* change automatically.

Most of my business or sales executive clients have had these two beliefs about mistakes and failure. And the type of parenting behaviour I described is typical of the source of the beliefs for almost all of them.

That's the Bad News... Here's the Good News

Beliefs like these and others can be very quickly and permanently eliminated. And what I've discovered from my work with clients is that as soon as these two beliefs are eliminated, (sometimes a few other core beliefs have to be eliminated) the fear of failure literally disappears forever. The best way to create your own reality, a world in which people are moving ahead rapidly as top performers, is to help yourself and others get rid of the beliefs that are preventing such behaviour in the first place.

Can you imagine living your life with no fear of rejection, criticism or failure at all? How different would your life be? It's totally possible today by eliminating all the beliefs that cause these patterns of behaviour-first.

"Nothing in life has any meaning except the meaning you give it."
– Tony Robbins

Truth #5 – Things that Happen have No Inherent Meaning

What exactly do I mean by this? Let's say for example you are leisurely travelling at 70mph in the middle lane of the M62 in your 3 year old, hard earned BMW 3 series, when all of a sudden; Wham! A brand new, straight out the showroom, diamond white Range Rover Vogue flies past you in the fast lane doing 100 mph and cuts right across your car, just in time to make it down the approaching slip road............

Your possible thoughts could be,

1. All people who drive Range Rovers are arseholes.

2. Blimey, I wish I had one of those beauty's.

3. I bet he's a drug dealer getting chased by the cops.

4. He's in a rush. Maybe his wife is just about to have a baby and needs to get to hospital sharpish?

5. Footballers wife. Probably left her handbag in Harvey Nicks.

6. Rich people don't care about anything or anybody other than themselves.

7. A hundred other "interpretations."

The point I'm making is that you don't know *anything* for sure. Based on that one "event" other than a white Range Rover driving past at 100mph, you know absolutely nothing about the person or their situation for definite. However, in that moment you are going to make a judgement about that situation, based on previously held beliefs about all the elements that made up that particular situation.

Whatever you decide to "interpret" about that situation in the moment changes the emotion you feel. Jealousy, angry, empathy, inspired or even nothing at all. As soon as you "pick" a choice, (mostly unconsciously) that choice then validates and confirms your already preconceived ideas. This leads us very closely to how the beliefs you have today have been previously formed.

Truth #6 – Change Can be Superfast, If You Know How

Most people don't believe this. Most people believe that "change is difficult and takes a very long time." This is understandable and is one of the first few beliefs that I or one of my trained associates need to eliminate for a client, in order for the rest of the **SHIFT B.E.L.I.E.F.S System™** to work effectively and for them to get the results they want.

The truth is that many people have gone to a gym for a while, tried to lose weight, decided to be more productive, gone to lots of seminars, read lots of books and still haven't changed. In fact, for some people the Triangle of Truth (illustrated on page 19) will only serve to validate their preconceived ideas about behavioural change. If they don't continue to read the rest of the book that is! Ironically, because the masses believe change is hard, they all tend to share and distribute their *war stories* of how hard things have been, in order for them to get what they want. There are no "hero miles" clocked up, no mileage in the "woe to win" story at the summer BBQ if change has been easy.......

When learning how to speak on stage and do presentations many speaker trainers will tell you, you need a good "hero's journey." A tale of how you "overcame adversity." They tell you that the audience will identify with this as they mostly believe that *"success is difficult"*(a very common limiting belief). This belief shows up in a thousand different places in the media. From soap operas to Hollywood films to autobiographies. In fact, if you look at nearly any successful Disney or Hollywood film, from the Lion King to Rocky, they all contain a very familiar script. Take a look at any successful film and you'll find the main characters having to triumph over adversity in some way.........all supporting more evidence of "woe to win" as a "fact" in the world.

In the area of which our discussion is based today, namely around fear, productivity and becoming a top performer the main reason for change being slow and difficult is because people haven't permanently eliminated the beliefs that are *causing* them problems in the first place! This is something that we are going to get into in more detail in Chapter 4.

Truth #7 – Success Information Doesn't Work

Many of my business clients have spent countless hours and have invested heavily in business and personal development programs either for themselves as individuals, or as part of trying to grow the business. The businesses I advise usually have a great team and are often getting good advice from consultants or coaches.

They are often parents as well and are always trying new ways to help their children grow up with high levels of self-esteem, confidence and happiness. The problem isn't a commitment to positive change. It's an inability to initiate and sustain it. Clearly we have discovered that the old methods aren't working. Many people are waking up to the realisation that they need an entirely new method of getting to the core of their problems, but they have little or no idea where to look.

The result of all this is deep cynicism-bordering on despair in some cases. A cynicism that has affected individuals, companies, parents and society as a whole - a sense of "What's the use? Things will never change anyway."

Many of my business clients have used business coaches or consultants for advice and support on how to change. I admire them for that because it demonstrates they are eager to be more effective either as a person, or to have a more successful business. But I have also seen that after years of self-help programs and excellent advice, these clients can still be stuck with their old ineffective actions and behaviours. Maybe they get results for a while, but they soon adopt the original ineffective patterns of behaviour. Often by the time they get to me they are understandably sceptical about how I can help them with the **SHIFT B.E.L.I.E.F.S System™**. Many are intrigued when they find out it's not NLP (Neuro-Linguistic Programming), hypnosis or some other Jedi mind trick voodoo. There is a really good reason why people are usually unable to change their own behaviour by conventional methods. The principles implicit in most attempts to change behaviour is,

Success Information + Motivation = **Change!**

This makes perfect sense to most people, whether they are training professionals, coaches or consultants, parents or individuals.

If you know what to do and how to do it, and are sufficiently motivated either by pain or reward, surely that is all that is needed to change behaviour and get the results - right?

Obviously not, since the formula of Success Information + Motivation doesn't seem to be working.

Let's take a simple example. Let's say you have good intentions-but somehow you always manage to keep on putting things off until the last minute. As a result your anxiety levels are constantly high much of the time and because of this behaviour, it's causing problems in your business or with your clients or customers.

You're in danger of losing a top client perhaps, one that is worth some serious money to you, but because you keep putting things off all the time, even the good relationship you currently have with them is starting to go a little bit sour. You decide you must change, and you really do *want* to change!

So this is what you do.

- You attend a webinar or seminar on productivity and read the 7 Habits of Highly Effective People.

- You prioritise your activities, assuming that it will help you focus on the most important tasks.

- You make a schedule that helps you allot time during the month for work on the project.

- You put up sticky post it notes as reminders next to your inspirational, "ATTITUDE" eagle flying high poster.

- You treat yourself with a vanilla slice from Greggs as a reward when you finish an item on the list.

So now you've gathered all the success information and resources you need to get your projects done on time and more importantly you have the motivation to do it. You also have the potential loss of income if you don't get it done, a happy client if you do get it done and a trip to the High Street for a sticky bun and alleviation of your anxiety to boot.

But be honest! After you've prepared yourself for this change and all the other variations of self-management you've discovered so far, does the behaviour pattern *really* change? Does the Success Information + Motivation strategy enable you to sit down *easily* and do what you said you were going to do? And even if it works temporarily, does it continue to work and be easy, month after month after month? For most, the answer is a big fat NO!

Think about ALL the times you've made a similar commitment based upon the Success Information + Motivation strategy but for some inexplicable reason you failed to follow through and you'll start to see a pattern emerging.

Let's say you need some new clients so you decide to go to a local networking event. You have to give a quick talk about you and your business but you are concerned about what other people think about you. That's common enough in my experience. You've decided your ever present concern with the perceived judgement and opinion of others is annoying at best, and prevents you from standing out in a crowded marketplace. You know that in order to succeed in today's competitive world you have to get in front of people who need and want what you sell.

Again, you really want to change. You think that if you can rid yourself of this problem you will be a lot more comfortable around people when explaining what you do and subsequently make more contacts and ultimately make more money. Maybe you read a book about feeling it and doing it anyway. Maybe you start shouting, "*I like myself, I like myself*" affirmations at the bathroom mirror in an attempt to psyche yourself up. You realise that the desire to be liked by everyone is impossible and if people don't like you, well that's just tough. Maybe you convince yourself that people who go networking aren't your kind of people, so it doesn't really matter anyway.

But don't you find, even with all your "positive thinking" and all your efforts, that the need to be liked by everybody doesn't really go away? The reason is simple enough:

Success Information + Motivation on their own aren't enough to change emotional and behavioural patterns, because the beliefs that CAUSE the patterns <u>haven't been eliminated first.</u>

The formula that's been peddled for decades doesn't work as effectively as people would have you believe because it never deals with your beliefs, so lasting change isn't possible. In many ways the situation gets worse because we con ourselves into thinking that Success information + Motivation *should* work and we blame ourselves or someone else when it doesn't. We think, "I'm incompetent" or "I don't have what it takes", "What's wrong with me?" Sales managers and bosses all across the UK think, "She'll never learn" or "What the hell's wrong with him?" or "Why doesn't she just bloody get on with it?"

If the beliefs *causing* the lack of implementation are eliminated first, all previously learned strategies for success, all past trainings and ideas are now called upon and implemented with enthusiasm and eagerness. Productivity is increased automatically and very often dramatically.

The main thing that has been stealing your success over the years is beliefs. We're going to sort out that problem in Chapter 4 but for now, read on and discover another piece of this success puzzle, what I call, "The Magic Genie..."

EXERCISES

What is the real cause of fear?

_____

_____

_____

_____

What do you fear most?

_____

_____

_____

_____

What are the only fears you are born with?

_____

_____

_____

_____

What's the most valuable idea you've learnt or re-learnt from this chapter?

_____

_____

_____

_____

Chapter 2

The Magic Genie

You ou were born with the most sophisticated and complex instrument the planet has ever known – your marvellous mind. Very few people have any concept of what the mind actually is, how to describe it, or how to alter it forever. Sure, everyone says you need to change your *mind*, but no one tells you exactly *how* to change it.

We were not born with a manual on how the mind works or how to maximise its use. Without this information, thousands of people wander through the deserted halls of dreams, always hoping, but rarely achieving. I believe we have now discovered one of the best concepts in the world today to describe the mind, how it works, and more importantly how to change it. The beauty of this model is that it is really easy to understand.

The Stickperson concept was developed in the 1930s by Dr. Thurman Fleet, the founder of Concept Therapy.

Dr. Fleet was a famous chiropractor who practiced in the first half of the 1900's in San Antonio, Texas. His practice was so busy that the city had to re-route traffic patterns in order to accommodate the people going to his office. His practice grew so fast that he had to move three times in order to conform with local fire hazard codes! His practice sometimes saw over 500 patients per day. The family members of

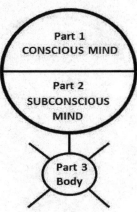

Figure 2

41

most of the prominent medical doctors in Texas at the time were Dr.Fleet's patients. People came to Dr.Fleet from all over the world to be helped from practically any dis-ease. The results that Dr.Fleet's patients achieved were unequalled at that time.

He came up with the notion that we actually live on three levels of existence: the Conscious Mind (**Part 1**) the Subconscious mind (**Part 2**) and the Body (**Part 3**). As we tend to think predominantly in pictures, Dr Fleet recognised the importance of having an image of the mind to work with. The problem being that nobody has ever seen the mind, so Fleet designed a picture for us to work with.

Part 1 - The Conscious Mind

This is the part of you that thinks. You have the ability to choose which thoughts you will entertain. This is the place where ideas are formulated. You bring information through your outside world into your mind, through your five senses. Your freewill resides here. All pain, pleasure, and limitation originate in the conscious mind. This part of your mind serves as a filter for what you will allow to be impressed into your subconscious mind.

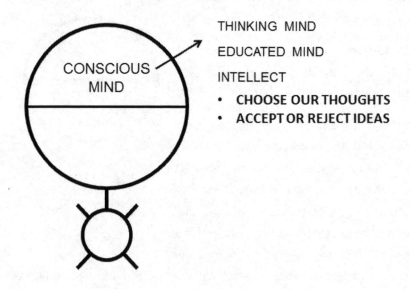

THINKING MIND

EDUCATED MIND

INTELLECT

- **CHOOSE OUR THOUGHTS**
- **ACCEPT OR REJECT IDEAS**

Figure 3

The conscious mind is made up of six mental muscles. Some people call these your higher faculties. It really doesn't matter what you call them. What's good to remember is that they are part of you, and you can develop and strengthen each one to create more awareness in your life and massively improve your results.

Perception

Is the ability to view your world differently. You can choose how circumstances will affect your life. You can develop much better ways to perceive your reality. One of the fastest ways to alter your perception is to eliminate the limiting beliefs that are not in harmony with the things you say you want to be, do and have.

Imagination

There is a power flowing into your mind that can allow you to create big ideas. The power of your imagination is one of the most powerful forces present in the world today. The ability to create new and better ideas is probably one of the most under-used and neglected tools and we have at our disposal. If you are like most people, this mental muscle gets squashed as you get older.

Will

This is the muscle that allows you to concentrate or focus. Most people are easily taken off course because they have never developed this mental muscle. You have the power right now to mentally focus on your goals and never get side-tracked irrespective of your current circumstances, environment, or situation.

Intuition

This is often referred to as your sixth sense. You have the ability to pick up information through your intuition in a way that is not yet fully explainable by modern science. Women believe they have a more highly developed sense of intuition than men, but men have developed it to a high degree as well.

Memory

You have a perfect memory. You never forget anything. You may need training as to how to retrieve it through your conscious mind, but it is perfect.

Reason

You can think and originate new and better ideas. You have the ability to accept or reject any thought; reason is what you use to decide. Many people choose to never use, let alone develop this mental muscle. It's a pity they don't. Their world would be very different if they did.

Imagine you come home one afternoon and find your front lawn littered with rubbish. If you are like most of us, chances are you would probably be upset; but you would still clean it up. During the clean-up you might wonder who on earth would want to do such a disgusting thing?

Now, imagine that the following afternoon you come home and again find your front lawn is littered with another truckload of rubbish. You'd probably be twice as angry as you were the evening before, but you would probably clean it up again, and start to wonder, *"Why would anyone want to do something like this?"*

Again, the next day, you come home and the front lawn is again littered with rubbish. This time you decide that you have had enough. You vow to put a stop to such disgusting destruction and aggravation. You would probably take whatever measures were necessary to stop this from continually happening.

Now, think of all the rubbish that is littered on the greatest "front lawn" in the world – your own mind. Most people continually allow rubbish to be dumped into their minds and refuse to do anything about it. The rubbish we are talking about is negative thinking. If we are not careful, it's very easy to allow others to pollute our minds.

So, you have to guard the front lawn of your mind. The tool to use is called reason. You can use your reason to accept or reject any ideas you want. You must not allow yourself to suffer from "stinking thinking." Be sure your mental guard is always on duty. You are responsible to ensure that he does his job properly.

Part 2 - The Subconscious Mind

This part of you is certainly the most powerful and magnificent. It is your power-centre. Every thought your conscious mind chooses to accept, this part must willingly accept. It has no ability to reject anything. As you'll see later this is really important when eliminating beliefs.

For every idea your conscious mind conceives, your subconscious mind will create whatever is necessary to fulfil that picture. If you have pictures of mediocrity in your conscious mind, then your subconscious mind will create exactly that, in reality, right on schedule.

All your prior conditioning from parents, authority figures and your own interpretations of life are found here. The subconscious mind is the emotional mind or "feeling mind." The ancient Greeks called it the "heart of hearts." It accepts all ideas presented uncritically and incorporates them into your beliefs.

The subconscious has no ability to reject thoughts. This is why you need to use your conscious mind to monitor thoughts and ideas as you receive them and close the door when negative thoughts are approaching. If you worry about something happening, then the subconscious will move you in the direction of having that negative thing happening. Likewise, if you create a positive idea of how you want things to unfold, like an inspiring and emotional goal, then the subconscious mind will internalise it and start working on the positive outcome you want in the same way.

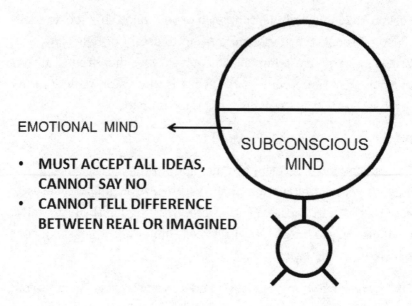

EMOTIONAL MIND

- **MUST ACCEPT ALL IDEAS, CANNOT SAY NO**
- **CANNOT TELL DIFFERENCE BETWEEN REAL OR IMAGINED**

Figure 4

The subconscious has no ability to tell the difference between the physical results on the outside or the images that you create with your imagination on the inside. This is highly important as it goes to work on whatever you feed it with.

Part 3 - The Body

This part of you is by far the smallest part of who you really are. This part is the part that expresses what is happening on the inside. Your body never lies-neither do your results.

Whatsoever is impressed on your mind will express itself on the physical plane of life through your body. Your body is an instrument of the mind; it materialises the exact images and beliefs impressed on the mind through repetition or emotion.

This involves behaviour. Behaviour and actions determine results. Want better results? Change your behaviour. Want better behaviour? Change the feelings and beliefs in your subconscious mind. How do you do that? Change the pictures in your conscious mind and eliminate all limiting beliefs preventing you from getting what you want. Let's keep it simple.

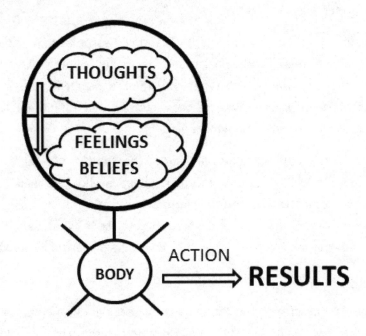

Figure 5

You either choose your thoughts or accept them from an outside source. These thoughts develop into images or ideas in your conscious mind. You then impress these images upon your subconscious mind, causing feelings and beliefs. These feelings and beliefs cause our actions and these actions create our results.

Our physical results on the outside, our health, relationships, and money we earn - all of our results, are the internal images and beliefs held in the subconscious mind continually expressing themselves through the body. If you want to change your behaviour and results permanently, we must change them on the inside-**first.**

The Farmer's Field

The conscious mind is like a farmer deciding what to plant in his field. The subconscious mind is like the farmer's field. It has no choice as to what will be planted. When the farmer plants a corn seed, corn grows in the field. When a carrot seed is planted in the farmer's field, the farmer will reap a carrot.

It would be foolish to think that by planting a carrot seed, a stalk of corn would emerge from the ground, yet many people believe this will happen in their lives. When you think a negative thought or concentrate on visions of failure, the results for you will ultimately be failure-by law it can't be anything else.

You decide which seeds you will plant by the thoughts you think. It is no more possible for you to think negative thoughts and reap positive results than it is for a farmer to plant a carrot seed and harvest corn. Some people have been careless in what they have planted over the years, and now they have a field overrun by weeds.

We need to clear the field and start re-planting.

Start planting images and thoughts of success right away, regardless of what your external results have dictated in the past. Get rid of your weed thoughts and soon you will have a rich and abundant harvest.

Just as the forces of nature turn an acorn into an oak tree, we can harness the same forces of the universe. Your subconscious mind utilises all of the forces of nature, outside of your awareness to produce results.

It is no more difficult to plant a seed of corn than it is to plant a weed seed. The subconscious is the servant of man; learn how to use it by giving it commands that will produce the results you want.

The Captain & Crew Concept

Here is a powerful concept. I want you to think of Part 1, your conscious mind, as the captain and Part 2, your subconscious mind, as the crew. People can direct their subconscious minds to eliminate doubt, create better results, and attract everything they need into their lives. How? By using the captain and crew concept.

The captain is your conscious mind. When you think of something, it is viewed as a command by the crew. The purpose of the crew is to fulfil all of the commands of the captain. So when you think, *"I'm so tired"* your crew interprets this as a command from the captain and produces "tiredness" in your body.

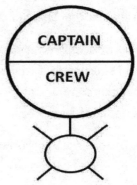

Figure 6

It can be scary, but think about this: Every thought you have becomes a command to the crew. Whatever you think, the crew will hear as an order and oblige the captain. Your crew is your subconscious mind and it exists to obey the captain. It responds instantly and automatically like clockwork. It is a law and it is always true. The crew responds to the captain's command. No matter what you say as the captain, the crew will interpret it as a command and move into action to make that thing happen. The crew only has a one word vocabulary and that word is *"YES."*

The crew has no ability to reject ideas. Whatever the captain says, the crew puts into action to produce in your life. It has no ability to say *"No."* In fact, it doesn't even respond to jokes at all. Many people repeatedly make statements such as, *"I'm terrible with names"* or *"my memory is getting worse!"* This causes a person to perpetuate the very thing they don't want!

The person making £30,000 a year is sending out thoughts to his crew that say "I am worth £30,000 a year," and that is what the crew produces by virtue of your actions. Every time you say anything it is interpreted as a command to the crew. You have to become extremely aware of what you say to yourself at all times. As I said previously, you and I live on three levels of existence simultaneously.

You are first and foremost a spiritual being, you have an intellect, and you live in a physical body. You're not a body, you just live in a body. You're not a brain, you use your brain. Who are you then, really? You are a spiritual being of consciousness and energy.

The most powerful part of you is non-physical. It is your conscious and subconscious minds. You have the power to originate thoughts, get the crew working on those thoughts and make an unbelievable amount of resources available to you, that are already-within you.

Most of us are locked into our physical awareness, but our physical bodies are the smallest part of our existence. We are in the habit of looking at our past results, such as how much money we earned last year, and we continue to let these results dictate the thoughts about how much we can make in the future. This is crazy!

We've got it totally backwards. We need to start originating the images we want to have happen in the future *now* and allow these images to be picked up by the subconscious. Let it do the work on your behalf by connecting you up with the entire universe.

This is the master power available to you, and you are using it right now. Use the power of your mind to take yourself to the next level. Everything starts as an image in your mind. Right now you are reading this and the thought of your ever becoming a millionaire might be so wild, so beyond your imagination it might almost make you laugh. Don't worry about it. Everything worthwhile starts out as a fantasy, a dream or an image. You can't have a Millionaire lifestyle with a twenty-quid head, so build the image of what you want right now, irrespective of what your currently experiencing.

If you hold on to an image long enough and start playing with it, it starts to turn into some theories about *how* you can do it. Theories that are worked on, developed and energised turn into facts. There is a power available to you in your mind, and if you use it, it will have a fantastic effect on your life. We are going to deliberately direct the power of our minds to produce much happier, wealthier lives for ourselves, our families and create a better world for everyone.

The Captain

So, your conscious mind is your captain. The captain gives orders to the crew, and it's their job to carry out every single order. They take their orders from the captain via thoughts. Whatever you think is interpreted as a command from the captain and the crew goes to work INSTANTLY to oblige the captain.

The Crew

Your subconscious mind is like your crew, which exists to obey your commands *instantly* and *automatically*. The crew has a one-word vocabulary. Whenever you, the captain, give a command, the crew always responds with the only word they know, and that word is... YES! Your subconscious mind is connected to your superconscious mind or infinite intelligence, and responds to the thoughts and feelings that you put out into the universe.

The Power of Choice

The beauty of being human is that we can reason and we can choose our thoughts. You can choose to create options and responses to produce wonderful results in your life. An animal receives stimulation and automatically responds. I know many people like that. They go through life and they are never, ever sure they have options. Life can be tough and beat you down if you let it. People just respond without thinking - without thinking that there are two sides to everything and that, as human beings, when we receive a stimulus from an outside source we have the ability to create options in our lives. You have the ability to choose the thoughts in your mind right now.

Before you reached the age of reason (around six years old) authority figures in your life were instrumental in implanting concepts into your mind which, upon further reflection you might want to reject.

We are now going into a section that will allow you to examine some of those concepts and show you how to quickly and permanently eliminate these ideas in order to overcome their impact on your life.

EXERCISES

What are the three parts of your personality?

_____

_____

_____

_____

How does your conscious mind differ from your subconscious mind?

_____

_____

_____

_____

Which is most powerful. Conscious or Subconscious? Why?

_____

_____

_____

_____

What do you say to yourself that limits you?

_____

_____

_____

_____

Chapter 3

Your Secret Blueprint

One of the most important but little known psychological discoveries of recent times is the discovery of the self-concept. By understanding your self-concept and by learning to manage and modify it to suit your purposes, you gain incredible self-confidence and power.

Whether we understand and realise it or not, each of us holds within us a mental blueprint or internal image of ourselves. For most people it may be blurry and ill-defined to our awareness, in fact it may not be consciously recognisable at all. This self-concept is the master program of your subconscious mind and continually produces your behaviour. This self-concept is our own made up system of the "kind of person I am." It has been built up over the years from our *beliefs* about ourselves.

Most of these beliefs have been unconsciously formed by past perceptions or interpretations about the events, environments and circumstances that we have been exposed to, especially during early childhood, but particularly up to the age of 6 years old. From all these interpretations about these external circumstances and events we subconsciously construct a *self* (or at least an image of a self). Once an idea or belief goes into this image it becomes our unique and individual "truth." Most behavioural and productivity problems we have today are driven by beliefs that we never challenge. We never question the validity of these individual beliefs that have made up this "concept" and therefore continually act just as if it *were true*. In the absence of any deliberate change on your part, you will continue doing, thinking, saying and feeling very much the same things indefinitely.

"The self-image controls what you can and cannot accomplish, what is difficult or easy for you, even how others respond to you just as certainly and scientifically as a thermostat controls the temperature in your home."
— Maxwell Maltz

The Snap-Back Effect

In the classic book Psycho-Cybernetics, Dr Maltz used the phrase the Snap-Back effect to explain the phenomenon of why we try to change, want to change but often don't.

The person that perceives themselves to not be cut out to be an entrepreneur or "not a salesman," will soon find some way to fail despite all his good intentions or striving. You cannot outperform or escape your self-image for long. If you do momentarily, you'll be "snapped back," like a rubber band extended between two fingers, coming loose from one. For the salesperson it could be one of the various aspects of the selling process. Maybe they are no good at finding new customers, developing relationships or consider themselves "no good at closing." You can however insert ANY specific into this, it's not just exclusive to business, it could be your golf game, public speaking or weight loss. The control by your self-concept is absolute and all encompassing. This snap-back effect is *universal.* All your actions, feelings, behaviour, even your abilities, are always consistent with this self-concept. As a result of this our external experiences seem to verify, confirm and strengthen this self-concept and either a viscous or beneficent cycle occurs. In other words the sales professional or entrepreneur will find that their actual experiences tend to "prove" that their self-concept is correct.

Whatever is difficult for you, whatever frustrations you have in your life, they are likely "proving" and reinforcing themselves because of beliefs and images lodged in your subconscious. Because of this external "proof" it seldom occurs to us that our trouble lies in this self-concept or our own evaluation of ourselves. You always act in a manner consistent with your self-concept, consistent with the bundle of beliefs you have acquired from infancy onward. In other words you are where you are and what you are because of what you believe yourself to be. Whether you are rich or poor, happy or unhappy, successful or unsuccessful it's your beliefs that are determining these outcomes. So if your self-concept is the real key to permanent and lasting change, where does it come from, how is it formed and most importantly how can you deliberately alter and reprogram it to dramatically increase your effectiveness in everything you do, and make change easy? Incredible changes have occurred both for the earning capacity of entrepreneurs and salespeople once they altered this concept of "self," *first*.

How Your Self-Concept Was Formed

You were not born with a self-concept. From a practical and understandable standpoint it is beneficial to understand that you were born **Tabula Rasa**, the real Latin translation meaning "scraped tablet," but is often translated in English to "blank slate." It is the notion that an individual human being is born "blank" (with no built-in mental content) and that their identity is defined entirely by events after birth. In terms of self-concept this is true, however, genetics obviously play a part in the full development and overall structure and make-up of the physical body and mind.

Thomas Aquinas was the first to assert the *tabula rasa* theory in the 13th century, though it was John Locke who fully expressed the idea in the 17th century. In John Locke's philosophy, *tabula rasa* was the theory that the human mind is at birth a "blank slate without rules," for processing information. These rules for processing are formed solely by one's physical senses and experiences. As understood by Locke, *tabula rasa* meant that the mind of the individual was born "blank", and it also emphasised the individual's freedom to author his or her own identity.

Each individual is free to define the content of his or her character. It is from this presumption of a free, self-authored mind combined with an immutable human nature that *Tabula rasa* is also featured in Sigmund Freud's psychoanalysis.

In recent times, however, *tabula rasa* has come to be understood fundamentally differently. Generally people now recognise the fact that most of the brain is indeed pre-programmed and organised in order to process sensory input, motor control, emotions and natural responses.

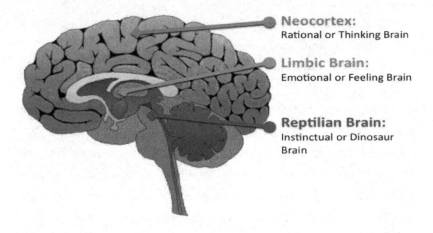

Neocortex:
Rational or Thinking Brain

Limbic Brain:
Emotional or Feeling Brain

Reptilian Brain:
Instinctual or Dinosaur Brain

Figure 7

These pre-programmed parts of the brain then learn and refine their ability to perform their tasks. The only true "clean slate" in the brain is the neo-cortex. This is the biggest part of the brain and is involved in thought and decision making (therefore decides upon interpretation and consequently your self-concept) and is strongly linked with the amygdala in the Limbic brain.

The amygdala is involved in responses such as fight or flight and emotions and like other parts of the brain is largely "pre-programmed", but has space to learn within its "programming." The amygdala is important in that it has a strong influence over the neo-cortex. There is much debate as to whether the amygdala prevents the neo-cortex from being defined as a clean slate. However, it affects emotions and not consciousness, so for our purposes of altering the self-concept it's not essential to know about.

Every attitude, behaviour, value, opinion and belief you have regarding yourself today has been learned, therefore if there are elements of your self-concept that do not serve your purposes, you can *unlearn* them. A good example of this is Chris Gardener.

Born on the 9th February, 1954 in Milwaukee, Wisconsin, Christopher Paul Gardner's childhood was marked by poverty, domestic violence, alcoholism, abuse and family illiteracy. Gardner published his autobiography out of a desire to shed light on these universal issues and to show people how they do not have to define you.

You might already know some of his story – if you watched the 2006 film, "The Pursuit of Happyness", starring Will Smith as Gardner. It documents the period of homelessness he suffered with his young son as he fought to become a stockbroker. He is now an entrepreneur, author and speaker.

Gardner's quick to put the film into context. *"The film was about one year of my life. I was 28 years old – there were 27 years before that."* Finding success, he says, is learning that you have choices.

"There's a school of thought that says you're a product of your environment. That means I would've become an alcoholic, wife-beating, child-abusing, illiterate loser. A lot of people would've said, 'well, look where he's from. He didn't have a choice.' But of course, I did have a choice."

In 1982, he passed his licensing exam and became a top earner at Bear Stearns, the New York based global investment bank. Five years later, armed with one piece of furniture – a desk – and just $10,000 of start-up capital, he left and started Gardner Rich, a brokerage firm that made him a multi-millionaire.

Much of Gardner's tenacity and determination came from his mum – a "light" during his childhood. He recalls announcing to her as a kid that, when he grew up, he was going to become the famous jazz musician, Miles Davis. She replied, "Son, there's only one Miles Davis, and he's got that job. You've got to be you."

Once you understand how your self-concept was formed, you will be able to bring about the changes that will make you into the kind of person you long to be and want to be like. You will learn how to become the kind of person who can accomplish the goals and dreams that are most important to you.

> *"Before you can do something you must first be something."*
> *– Goethe*

Children come in to the world with no self–concept at all. Children learn who they are and how important and valuable they are (or aren't) by the way they are treated daily and the subsequent "interpretations" they make about the events that happen around them. Naturally, infants also have an incredible inbuilt desire for love, touching and holding.

Children need love like they need oxygen. The emotional healthiness of the adult will largely be determined by the quality and quantity of love and affection the child receives predominantly from the parents or primary caretakers.

A child that was raised with an abundance of love and emotional support during the formative years generally grows up to be well balanced and mostly positive. A child that is raised with criticism and punishment will tend to grow up fearful, sceptical and with the potential for a variety of personality and behavioural problems that continue to manifest in later life.

The Pleasure Principle

As we mentioned in Chapter one, children are only born with three fears: Loud noises, falling and abandonment. All other fears have to be taught by **repetition and reinforcement** while the child is growing up.

The second remarkable quality of children is that they are completely *uninhibited.* They say and do exactly what they feel like with no concern at all for the opinion of others. They are completely spontaneous and express themselves fully and naturally with no inhibitions at all. The great thing about this is that being completely fearless, unafraid of anything or anyone is your *natural* state. Free to express your opinions and beliefs in the world freely and easily in all situations is how you are meant to live.

Children learn behaviour in two fundamental ways. First by imitation of one or both parents. Many of your adult habit patterns, including your values, your attitudes and beliefs were formed by watching and by listening to your parents when you were growing up. Often a child will identify more strongly with one parent and will be more influenced by that parent than the other.

The other main way that children learn is by moving away from pain to pleasure, by moving away from discomfort towards comfort. Sigmund Freud called this the "pleasure principle." His conclusion, and that of most psychologists, is that this striving toward pleasure or happiness is the basic motivation for all human behaviour. There is a continuous drive *toward* what feels good and *away* from what feels bad.

Of all the discomforts that a child can suffer, the real or perceived withdrawal of love and approval of the parent is one of the most traumatic and frightening. Children have an intense burning desire for their parents love, support and protection. When a parent deliberately withdraws his or her love in an attempt to control behaviour or discipline the child, the child becomes extremely uncomfortable and insecure.

The interpretation of the child is everything. It is not what the parents meant or intended that counts, it is what the child *perceives* that affects the child's beliefs, feelings and actions. When the child perceives that love has been withdrawn, the child immediately changes his or her behaviour in an attempt to win back the parents love and acceptance.

Because of the "pleasure principle" there is a natural striving for the child to conform to the parents demands and requirements in order to prevent the feeling of love withheld. Frustrated and confused, the child eventually loses his or her natural fearlessness and spontaneity. The mediocrity that continues into adult life, begins.

The Starting Point of Belief

Let's take a pretty typical example of everyday happenings in a family household of let's say, three kids.

Assume that you are a three-year old child, the second of three. You are the middle child and you have a very young baby sister and an older brother of six years old. Your parents have never smacked you or yelled at you. Your dad works all day, and your mother stays home to take care of you and your siblings.

When you wake up in the morning, you jump out of bed and you say "Mummy, Mummy, play with me, draw with me, read to me." Mummy, who also works from home, is busy looking after your baby sister and trying to get the six year old dressed, fed breakfast and into the people carrier all at the same time. So your Mum replies, "Not now darling, I just need to feed the baby and get your brother to school. Maybe later, I'm busy at the moment."

Imagine that similar scenes get repeated every hour or so until 6 pm when Daddy comes home. You rush to the door and yell, "Daddy,

Daddy, play with me Daddy, look at what I made you today!" And Daddy replies, "Ok, Ok , just give me a minute to get my coat off, get through the door and relax a second, will you!"

Ten minutes pass and again you ask again, "Please Daddy, play with me?" Again Daddy replies, "Yes I will, I promise, I just need to go and have a shower first, and then I will."

Eventually, Dad spends a few minutes with each of the kids, reads the paper and watches TV, followed by dinner. If you're lucky maybe you got some playtime before you had to go to bed, maybe you didn't.

So what happened on this typical day of your life at age three? You asked for attention fifteen or maybe twenty times, and almost every time you heard, "No, not now." Even if we were being conservative and said you asked for attention six times a day, that would mean about two thousand requests in a year that were usually denied, and over six thousand separate denials by the age of six! Now here's the six million dollar question:

What meaning or interpretation are you *likely* to conclude given these experiences with your Mum or Dad?

If you're a typical child, you might conclude (unconsciously) **I'm not important.** That would be a natural and normal conclusion for a small child at that age. You have had thousands of separate incidents that you didn't understand and that probably upset you. But deciding **I'm not important** now allows you to make sense of them. If you're not important, of course Mum and dad wouldn't have time for you.

Say you carry this unconscious conclusion into your adult life (that's what usually happens) and at some point you decide that the only way you are going to really succeed is to run your own business. It goes reasonably well for a year or two but after a while you start to get frustrated because all the marketing guys tell you if you are really going to make a huge success of your business, you have to put yourself out in to the world-big time. Just the thought of this starts to make you fearful. Why? Because of all of the beliefs you have "learnt" about yourself as a child, swim to the top of your consciousness like goldfish in a tank at feeding time, and make you *feel* anxiety.

This is of course is just one of many beliefs people have unconsciously decided that are "true" about themselves. This is the *real* reason people put things off and procrastinate, fear speaking in public, find it hard to make changes and have many fears outside the genetic fears we are born with, including the big three fears of rejection, failure and criticism.

Consider another example of how your beliefs determine your behaviour. Assume you held this belief: **The way to succeed in life is to avoid mistakes.** Although this belief doesn't necessitate any specific behaviour, it would undoubtedly limit your behaviour in one or more of the following ways:

- You would avoid taking chances.

- You would do the same thing, day after day, believing that if it worked yesterday it will work today.

- You would be more interested in blaming someone or something else for a mistake than finding the source and correcting it.

- You would resound defensively to criticism.

Behaviour that is incompatible with your beliefs - like being open to criticism or taking risks-would be highly unlikely. Your behaviour occurs in the box defined by your beliefs.

Usually there are a combination of beliefs that contribute to a pattern of behaviour.

Steve, a client of mine who was in sales, came to me because he knew he had to make a lot of presentations in public and had to really put himself out in to the marketplace in order to be a top performer in his industry. Some of the beliefs we uncovered were, **Mistakes and failure are bad; If I make a mistake or fail I'll be rejected; what makes me good enough is having people think well of me; success is difficult and takes a long time.** The patterns in Steve's life could easily be explained by these and other related beliefs.

Helen had a problem with being identified as a leader in her network marketing business. This would of course mean having a lot of attention put on her, being on stage and the responsibilities that come with a higher position. What beliefs could cause this to be a problem? **It's dangerous for people to put their attention on me, I'm not worthy of success, I'm not good enough.** The interesting thing about limiting beliefs is that virtually no-one escapes. Everyone for the guy sweeping the floor in the basement of your local corner shop to the chief executive of a major plc in the city of London.

The reason that this is true is not only my experience of directly working with a wide range of clients, but simply because of how our minds function. Virtually all self-concept beliefs were formed at an age when you lacked the awareness and cognitive capacity to "choose." Your full range of conscious faculties had not yet been fully developed, you were pure emotion, so give yourself a break-you were just a kid.

What makes the **SHIFT B.E.L.I.E.F.S System™** so powerful is that your self-concept is subjective not objective. Your beliefs about yourself, especially your self-limiting beliefs and doubts are not based on fact at all. Negative ideas about yourself and your abilities are usually based on false information and impressions you have taken in and accepted as true. Let me explain.

In Figure 8, let the outside ring represent a physical "event" that actually took place. The thing that actually physically happened when you were a child for example. The middle ring represents the "interpretation" you gave that event, and the bulls-eye in the middle or centre ring is the emotion you "felt" at that time, based on the interpretation.

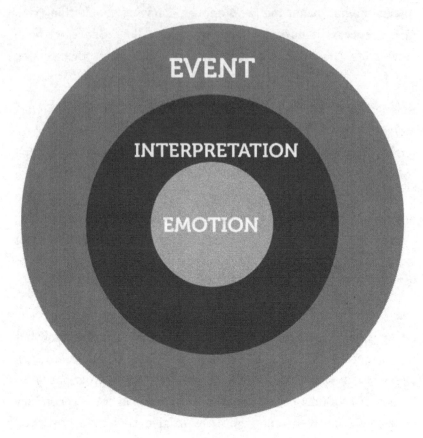

Figure 8

If we take the example of normal family life we gave earlier, such as not getting attention, it would go something like this.

EVENT FACT: I didn't get the attention I wanted.

INTERPRETATION/BELIEF: I'm not important.

EMOTION: Feeling not important.

But here's the thing; in this case, it IS a fact that you didn't get the attention you wanted, most kids don't, they want 24/7 attention generally, this IS a fact. However, if you had given this exact same event (and many other similar events) a different meaning or interpretation other than "I'm not important" when you were very young, would you have felt the same way? Let's find out. Other interpretations could include,

- Mam and Dad are just busy, it had nothing to do with me and my importance.

- Maybe I wasn't important as a kid, that doesn't mean as an adult.

- Maybe Mam and Dad were lacking in parenting skills and their behaviour had nothing to do with my importance.

- Maybe Mam and Dad were just acting out of beliefs about parenting that were passed down to them, and couldn't have acted any different, it had nothing to do with my importance.

- Maybe Mam and Dad were just stressed with having to pay bills and had to work a lot, it had nothing to do with my importance.

Now we have five different interpretations of exactly the same event, (You not getting enough attention) so the real question is, is "I'm not important" a FACT, or is it just one interpretation of many different interpretations that your mind could have come up with *at the time*? Really think about this. Nothing has ANY meaning in the world until we give it one. Why is the interpretation "I'm not important" ANY more valid than the other five above? Because it is, isn't an answer!

The reason you have any self-limiting belief holding you back today is because you repeatedly thought you *saw* it (and subsequently felt it) in the world as a fact. The truth is you did see the actual event or thing happening in front of you as a child, BUT you *chose* one interpretation out of multiple choices that were just as valid. They just didn't occur to you at the time because of your lack of awareness at that young age. Because you lived in the land of the giants so to speak, where it appears parents know exactly what to do, when to do it and how to do it, you concluded that the things that happened around you must be about you. You desperately wanted to make sense of your world so the most natural thing in the world was to point the finger at yourself.

Interpretation x Emotion x Repetition = BELIEFS!

Your beliefs don't come from what happened, they come from what you *interpreted* about what happened. Big difference. I made this distinction one day after talking to two sisters who grew up with an alcoholic father. One lady chose her relationship with her dad as a reason to never drink alcohol, whilst her sister who also turned into an alcoholic, blamed her father for her drinking. Both were exposed to the same EVENTS but interpreted them differently. This isn't about blaming anyone, especially your parents. They were for the most part just acting out of their beliefs, awareness and skills as a parent. They did the best they could with the knowledge they had at the time.

As soon as you begin to really think about these things and go through the entire process in Chapter 4, the beliefs and fears that have had such strong hold over you for so long will simply fall away.

When you begin to reject these self-limiting ideas, they lose their power instantly. It's like releasing the handbrake on a car one click at a time until you move forward freely and automatically.

Many people come to me for help because they simply know they should be much further ahead in their business or organisation, given the knowledge and talent they have compared to others.

Richard was no different. He worked in network marketing where positivity and productivity is everything. With time and effort the rewards can be incredible. I asked him what he thought the problem was and to monitor his thoughts and actions over a week or two.

In an email he replied,

"I want to be a recognised leader and have fun, but I fear I really don't have what it takes to be a leader and be taken seriously. I'm afraid of pissing anybody off. I'm too much of a people pleaser.

I am very knowledgeable (virtually an expert) on the topic of network marketing and keep learning, but don't execute... I'm stuck in the safe haven of 'learning and growing'. I also learn various conflicting methods from the top leaders and don't know which to run with, so I do nothing and use that as my excuse for inaction.

I don't push opportunities far enough - if I get some success then I feel 'that's my lot' whereas other people will push and push and push and maximise it.

I spend (far) too much time messing around on Facebook. Checking it at every opportunity. I don't even know why. I want to delete Facebook to stop an old habit, but I'm really afraid I will lose a lot of contacts..

I don't associate with enough leaders who will bring me up. Friends all earn less than I do. They are pulling me down. I buy into their excuses, way of thinking, and if I hang around with them too often I know this affects me.

I think people won't look up to me as a leader / respect me. Why would they? I want to be everyone's friend.

I'm afraid to have difficult conversations and look people in the eye at the same time. However, I am excellent at building rapport quickly and have open and honest conversations with people who I hardly know.

I am a starter, not a finisher.

I don't see things through, get the job done.

I run out of steam easily.

I think of any excuse not to finish, start, really experience success. I procrastinate and slow down, mess around, Facebook. Excuses every time. There is always something, when I'm on the verge of something big.

I always leave important things to the last minute and don't do a good enough job because I haven't given myself enough time.

I don't feel I deserve it or can handle being that successful.

One of the biggest drivers to a network marketing company is getting people to events. I'm afraid of handling/managing lots of people. Expectations, no shows, I always imagine I'm going to be let down. I need to feel I am capable of organizing huge volumes of people. Something always blocks me here. I am more than capable of doing it really......."

Within Richard's email were multiple patterns of behaviour which had to be unravelled to get individual patterns. However, it's often the same beliefs that cause multiple but different patterns.

Can you see how some of the beliefs I identified in our session together could contribute to Richards behaviour? *I'm not good enough, what makes me good enough is having people think well of me, I'm not important, life is difficult, I'll never get what I want.*

Realistically if anybody had these beliefs as "truths" in the world, would any **Success Information + Motivation** strategy really work? No, of course not. And this is the problem for so many people. Most of the time we know what to do, but our beliefs stop us from doing it.

Money, Money, Money

Within your overall self-concept you have hundreds of different specific mini-self concepts. These parts of your self-concept control your performance and your behaviour in each individual area of your life that you consider important.

You have a self-concept for how much you eat, how much you exercise or how fit you are. You have a self-concept of how attractive and sexy you are, how funny and popular you are and how good you are in your career or business.

If you are in sales for example, not only do you have an overall self-concept of yourself as a salesperson, but you also have individualised self-concepts for each area within the selling process. You have a self-concept for how good you are at rapport building, asking questions, identifying needs and so on. In each of these areas you will be relaxed or tense depending upon your beliefs and how you *think* of yourself in each of these areas.

You have a self-concept of how efficient you are, how organised you are and where you should "fit in." The most important discovery of our times is that you will always behave in a manner consistent with your self-concept. You cannot out-perform it for long. The Snap-Back effect prevails.

The Snap-Back effect causes real problems for entrepreneurs and salespeople, especially when it comes to the area of money. If you earn more than 10 percent above or below your self-concept you start to experience a certain level of anxiety, and begin engaging in compensatory behaviour. If you earn too much you begin to spend the money, or start investing in things you know little about-or just plain lose it. There are many stories to verify people winning large amounts of money, but very quickly disposing of it, only to return to where they were financially in a very short time.

If you earn 10 percent or more below your self-concept level of income you begin to engage in "scrambling" behaviour. You begin to think of ways to get your income back up to where it "should be." You start to work harder or longer, or you implement a marketing strategy that would drive more customers through the door in order to keep you in line with your self-concept-but only enough until the pain subsides and then you back off again and start coasting.

Everybody would like to have more money and the time to enjoy it, but when an opportunity comes along that will provide them with the chance, most people ignore it.

This reminds me of a story I once heard: An old grandfather was sitting on the porch in a rocking chair with his old hound-dog curled up beside him.

Every so often the old dog would wriggle around to get more comfortable and every time he did, he let out a baleful howl then would settle back down. One day, grandfather and hound-dog were sitting there when his young grandson came to visit and sure enough, the hound wriggled around gave out a baleful howl then settled back down. "Grandad," said the boy, "Why does he howl like that, is he hurt?" "Well son," said Grandad, "Underneath where the dog is resting is an old rusty nail, and every time he wriggles to get comfortable the nail digs into him." The boy thought for a moment and then said, "Why doesn't he just move then?" "I guess it just doesn't hurt enough," said Grandad."

I am sure this story relates to a lot of people who are searching for 'THE OPPORTUNITY.' It arrives and they realise that they now have to make the choice of staying right where they are (on the nail so to speak), or doing what is required and get off their arse to seize the opportunity. When this opportunity occurs the majority of people decide that the 'rusty nail' is really not that bad and choose to settle for what they have. Unfortunately, the perceived risk is just too high.

It is sad really, but over 82 percent of our population dislike their job yet they spend most of their lives there, 9–5 or even longer, Monday through Friday, we are talking 40–45 years. It is nothing but a treadmill. Sure it puts food on the table, pays the mortgage and bills but for the majority it is a treadmill that they are too frightened to change or get off. Wouldn't you like the opportunity to achieve the income you desire and the time to enjoy it? Don't keep sitting on that rusty nail then!

Your Triune Self Concept

Your self-concept is made up of three parts like layers of a wedding cake. The first part is your *self-ideal*. This is the ideal description of the person you would most like to be in every respect. Your self-ideal is a combination of the qualities and attributes that you admire most in yourself and others. It is the total of your dominant aspirations. Top performers have very clear self-ideals towards which they continue to move towards. Bottom feeders don't. Top performers are goal orientated and are continually moving towards what they want and how to get it in the shortest and most effective way. Bottom feeders aren't. The more clear you are about who you are and the person you ideally want to become the more likely you will evolve into that person.

The second part of your self-concept is your *self-image*. Your self-image is the way you *see* yourself and *think* about yourself in your daily activities. Your self-image is crucial to your performance in every area of your life that you consider important. You always act and behave consistent with this self-image. Because of this basic fundamental human trait, changing your beliefs at the identity level of understanding is one of the fastest ways to change performance. You always behave consistently with the picture you hold of yourself on the inside. Your self-image is often called the "inner mirror." This inner mirror reflects back to you how you are conditioned to behave in a given set of circumstances. Because of this you can instantly improve your results in any area of your life by deliberate modification of the self-image.

It is not possible to feel really good about yourself and perform poorly, nor is it possible to perform poorly and feel good about yourself. The more consistent your actions are with the very best person that you can imagine yourself becoming, your self-ideal, the higher will be your self-liking, self-respect and in turn your self-esteem.

The World Takes You at Your Own Evaluation

The third part of your self-concept is your *self-esteem*. Your self-esteem is how you *feel* about yourself. Your self-esteem is best defined as how much you like yourself. The more you like yourself, accept yourself and respect yourself as a valuable and worthwhile person, the higher your self-esteem is. The more that you feel that you are an excellent human being, the more positive and happy you are.

Your self-esteem determines your level of energy, enthusiasm and self-motivation. Your level of self-esteem is the control valve on your performance and effectiveness. Your self-esteem is like the fuel in the first and second stages of a rocket blasting off from Cape Canaveral. People with very high self-esteem do very well at everything they attempt.

The more that your day-to-day activities and goals are consistent with the person you want to become, the higher is your self-esteem. If your ideal is to be well-organised, calm, positive and working progressively toward the achievement of your goals, and in reality, you *are* behaving in a well-organised, calm, positive manner, working step-by-step toward your objectives, you will have a high, healthy level of self-esteem. You will like and respect yourself more. In turn others will respond favourably to this personality type simply because the world takes you at your own evaluation of yourself. You will feel calm and confident. You will feel happy, healthy and optimistic. You will have a high-performance personality.

Self-esteem is the foundation key of a positive self-concept. High self-esteem and self-acceptance are the critical elements in sales success. The more you like and respect yourself, the better you perform at everything you do.

Eliminating any beliefs that prevent high levels of self-esteem is the most important thing you can do, every day, in building yourself to the point where you are capable of achieving all your goals. The performance-based factor within self-esteem is self-efficacy. It's how competent and capable you feel you are in whatever you do. This is the bedrock upon which real and lasting self-confidence is built. People with high levels of self-esteem get along with just about everyone.

When you learn to deliberately modify this self-concept, which you will do through the **SHIFT B.E.L.I.E.F.S System™**, you'll walk, talk, act and perform at much higher levels than ever before automatically, simply because you are making a change at the core of who you are, at the identity level of self-concept.

PYRAMID OF PERFORMANCE^{TM}

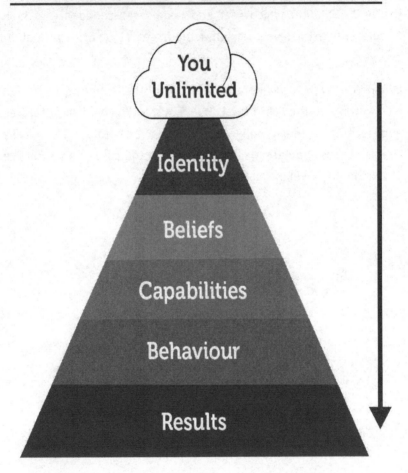

Figure 9

As you can see in the above diagram inspired by Robert Dilts, the Pyramid of Performance™ is very helpful in constructing a visual action plan for change. The stages of change give us a general road map of the *process* of change - a process that has a beginning, a middle and an outcome.

Gregory Bateson, a well-known English cultural anthropologist pointed out that in the processes of learning, change, and communication there were natural hierarchies.

The function of each logical level in the hierarchy was to organise the information below it. Changing something on a lower logical level of the hierarchy could, but *would not necessarily* affect the levels above it. However, making a change at an upper level *would* change everything below it and have a cascading effect in order to support that higher level change.

In other words, whatever is on top runs everything underneath. So if you make a change at a lower level but your problem is really at a *higher* level, then it will do little or nothing to change the areas above it. Change is unlikely to last – we always, "Snap-Back." When you fully understand this model it becomes obvious that the higher the level you make the change at, the more natural, automatic and powerful the change that you create will be. Change is and can be fast and effortless when you decide to change at the level of identity and belief. These areas are the *real* cause of all your results.

Negative Habit Patterns (NHP)

As we've seen there is a one to one relationship between your own self-concept and your potential as a human being. In each of us there are many areas of self-concept. One of the most important is our own human interactions with others. As well as eliminating beliefs, your self-concept can be built up by unconditional love, acceptance, and your attitude towards yourself. Conditional love diminishes your self-concept. Dominant parents often use the child's love to satisfy their own needs, greatly affecting the child's self-concept.

The result of a diminished self-concept is negative expressions, which lead to what is referred to as "Negative Habit Patterns." Along with limiting beliefs your NHP's are the primary cause of your limitations.

There are two kinds of negative habit patterns, **inhibitory** and **compulsive.**

A common mistake many parents make is the practice of destructive criticism with their children. Even in fun or teasing this can transmit to a child that their self-worth and behaviour are one and the same thing. The child then begins to associate their sense of self and their estimation of their own value as an individual, with their parents opinion of how they are conforming to *their* standards.

When destructive criticism is practiced repeatedly by the parent as a normal behavioural response, the child suffers psychic discomfort which can limit the child's performance indefinitely.

Inevitably this treatment robs the child of their individuality, saps their inner strength and lowers their chances of reaching their full potential.

Thoughts that indicate the presences of inhibitory NHPs are, "I can't, I wish I could, If only..." This feeling of "I can't" soon crystallises and contributes to the fear of failure. It's brought about by being told over and over again as a child, "NO! Stop that! Get away from there! or Put that down!"

Children by nature are curious and inquisitive. They do not understand why parents respond this way. All they understand is that whenever they try to do something, their parents respond negatively. Children interpret these negative responses as a result of being neither capable or worthy of praise.

Because it is not possible for children to differentiate between valid and invalid criticism at a very young age, they grow up with this NHP well ingrained.

The second major type of NHP that children learn is the *compulsive.* The compulsive negative habit pattern is learned by the child when parents make their love *conditional* upon the child's performance or behaviour. It's learned for example when parents say things like, "If you don't stop doing that, you're going to be in big trouble." A child interprets "trouble" as the withdrawal of love and approval.

The compulsive negative habit pattern develops because the child interprets and internalises the actions of the parents as "love withheld" or withdrawn, which in turn activates the third fear, the fear of criticism.

In a child's mind its typical to believe, "Unless I do what Mummy or Daddy tell me to do, I'm not safe and they might leave me, therefore I *have* to do what they want." "I have to, I have to, I have to...."

Thoughts that indicate compulsive NHPs are "I must... I have to be" and "You must." You can tell whether you interpreted this pattern because of the way you feel as an adult. You will be overly concerned with the opinions of others, especially of those close to you like your parents, spouse, boss or certain friends. This fear of criticism can be just as paralysing as failure and rejection. It can render you virtually incapable of making any major decision until you have it "rubber stamped," or you receive the approval of someone, especially in an position of authority.

The truth is that whatever love you did get or didn't get at the time had nothing to do with you. You were just a kid and people can't give away what they haven't got themselves.

Businesses obviously have a self-concept as well, as does each department within the business. If you are a small business owner or entrepreneur, your self-concept is reflected in your own personal brand, how you deal with people and how you think you are supposed to act in a business environment. How you act on a day to day basis has much more to do with your *internal* programming than it ever does with the *external* environment itself.

EXERCISES

What is the Snap-Back Effect?

_____

_____

_____

_____

What is Your Self-Concept?

_____

_____

_____

_____

How is Your Self-Concept formed?

_____

_____

_____

_____

What are the two major types of negative habit patterns?

_____

_____

_____

_____

Chapter 4

The SHIFT B.E.L.I.E.F.S SYSTEM™

Many behavioural experts including Tony Robbins, Bob Proctor and many more have argued that permanent change is virtually impossible without first eliminating the beliefs that keep us stuck. Many people have tried and bought programs that claim to eliminate beliefs, but unfortunately they have not been able to permanently eliminate beliefs that have been sabotaging their success for so long. As a result many people have naturally become sceptical that it really is possible. I mean how can you really change twenty, thirty, or even forty years or more of accumulated "bad programming" in about twenty minutes? Well, it can be done. Once an individual gets into the rhythm of the process and understands how it works, then twenty minutes is about the average length of time it takes in live client sessions for each belief to be permanently eliminated.

In this chapter I'm going to give you the very same system I use with my clients to permanently eliminate limiting beliefs. As you will see in this chapter, the **SHIFT B.E.L.I.E.F.S System™** (see Figure 10) usually requires the assistance of a trained facilitator when it is used to unravel complex behavioural patterns. This is mainly because in many complex patterns all of the beliefs are not known and there are specific skills to identify all of the beliefs that complete a full pattern. As we said earlier in the book, beliefs are usually unconscious and therefore tricky to identify yourself. However, as I will demonstrate once you know the beliefs you want to eliminate, you can use this process to eliminate limiting beliefs of your own and of your family, team or associates.

Figure 10

There are seven steps to the system as follows,

- **B**ehavioural or Emotion change wanted.

- **E**stablish beliefs responsible.

- **L**ocate the source of the belief.

- **I**nterpretation of alternatives.

- **E**vents have no meaning.

- **F**eeling Aspect of the belief.

- **S**ay the belief out loud.

Step 1 – Identify Behavioural or Emotional Change Wanted

I've chosen my client Sarah to help illustrate how the process works in reality. She heard me talking at a seminar about the power of the subconscious mind and how our beliefs are responsible for our performance. In short she thought I could help her.

Sarah's Story

Sarah had been working in her own business for three years and although she was doing okay, deep down she knew with all of her talent, knowledge and skill she could be doing so much better.

She was self-employed as a marketing consultant and was moderately active in helping small businesses market their products and services more effectively.

I asked Sarah to describe an undesirable pattern that she wanted to change.

She told me, "My problem is this. Although I have a lot of experience in marketing, I'm struggling to really put myself out there so that the right people know I exist. I go to a couple of local business networking groups but to be honest, I feel as though the people who attend are not really my target market. They aren't really big enough to afford my services so if I do get any interest from someone, I always have to drop my prices in anticipation of them rejecting what I have to offer."

"Is there anything else?" I asked.

She nodded.

"Yes, when I have to do a quick ten minute presentation to my networking groups, or even when I have to stand up and tell people what I do in front of a group of people, I can feel my heart racing. It starts to thump like it's going to come through my chest. In fact it can get that bad sometimes that I'm not really listening to the people speaking before me because of the anticipation of me having to speak after them."

"So what are the consequences of this, in your opinion?" I asked.

"Well, It's really, really frustrating because I know I am good at what I do but I don't assert myself and it looks like I'm lacking confidence. People pick up on this lack of confidence as an indication of my skills I guess. I know people who aren't as smart or as talented as me, but they often get the business because they appear self-assured to the clients. It's really pissing me off. Sometimes I really do consider just jacking it all in and going back to get a job. Being self-employed on your own is tough."

"Well, there are multiple patterns within what you have told me, which is the most important for you to work on first?" I replied.

"If we can stop the anxiety and fear I get when speaking in public then I think that would help enormously with my confidence. From that, people would probably see me in a new light and start to believe that I really can deliver what I say I can."

"So, fear of speaking in public is the first thing you'd like to work on?" I asked.

"Yes," she replied.

Step 2 – Establish Beliefs Responsible

I explained to Sarah that virtually everything we do and feel is a combination of beliefs, interpretations and conditioned behaviour. (For now though we are just going to look for possible beliefs that could explain her pattern).

"So, what do you believe in your mind that could account for your fear and anxiety, given that you weren't born with it?" I asked.

"If I'm being honest, even though I'm good at what I do, I doubt myself. I have the flashy car, business cards and website but when

I'm in front of people I get really anxious. I guess at some level **I don't feel good enough** and that's why I don't go after the bigger jobs as well. Sometimes I feel that **people aren't interested in what I have to say** in the networking groups. I feel that everyone's only interested in promoting themselves."

"Ok, so which of these two seems bigger than the other at the moment?"

She thought for a moment. **"I'm not good enough**.... hell, I *really* hate saying that, I feel like a fraud, but it feels so true."

"I understand that, I replied. Many people feel embarrassed about admitting to believing that they're not good enough. However, in my experience its very rare to *not* grow up believing this at some level based on how we form beliefs when we are a kid. Can you see how the belief **I'm not good enough** would at least partially explain your fear of speaking in public?"

"Yes, I can definitely see that it could," Sarah agreed.

Step 3 – Locate the Source of the Belief

I then asked Sarah to look inside her mind for the earliest circumstances or events that led her to form this belief, **I'm not good enough.** I went on to explain that most self-concept beliefs are formed before the age of six, based on early interactions with our parents or guardians at that time. Beliefs are usually formed by multiple events not just a single one-off incident, unless it's got some strong emotional component to it like seeing someone being shot or attacked.

At first she had a bit of difficulty identifying what exactly was the source of the belief. This is common, most people have never been asked the question or indeed ever consciously singled out the source of a limiting belief. So when I asked Sarah what might have happened that could have led her to form the belief, **I'm not good enough,** she told me about growing up on a small farm house in Yorkshire, with an older brother.

"I have an older brother David, and he has always been considered the 'clever one.' Whenever David did something well at school he used to get praise from Dad. Dad thought highly of doing well at school and held it in pretty high regard. I was always considered the 'creative one,' a bit more arty and playful. I used to love drawing and painting but in his eyes that wasn't considered worth pursuing in the same way. When I was about three my Dad started a new business. He was often up and down the country, working long hours in order to get the business started. A favourite expression of his that I remember to this day was, 'Business first.' I remember him being home at weekends, but was often reading up on business stuff or fixing something on the farm that needed repairing. Most weekends my brother and I would have to go and stay at Grandmas house, so that Mam and Dad could get on with the farm work."

"My parents were happy together, and Dad would often bring Mam something back, like a present if he'd been away somewhere, but my brother and I didn't seem to be as important. I guess during the first seven years of growing up I didn't really see that much of my Dad. He was always away on business or doing up the farm. I guess I never really knew him. He didn't really play with us that much as he was too busy with other stuff or just tired from working all the time."

"My Mam was always telling me to be a 'good little girl.' She never really praised me for anything or hugged me. It seems ridiculous to me now because I tell my own daughter, Chloe, that I love her all the time. I can't ever remember my Mam ever telling me once that she was proud of me. We were the type of family that just got on with stuff I guess, and we were brought up like that."

I had been listening without interruption for quite some time when I said,

"I think you've probably identified the source of the belief. Does it make sense to you now that what you've just told me about growing up is the source of the belief **I'm not good enough** and probably other beliefs as well?"

"After all, you weren't *born* with any limiting beliefs right?"

"Yes, said Sarah, I can see that now."

"Can you see that you were only very young and you were trying to make sense of your world. Trying to understand the confusing and sometimes painful emotions you felt? What happens subconsciously, is that your young mind is trying to make sense of all the different events going on around you. Unconsciously you made the distinction, **I'm not good enough.** As soon as you did that, as soon as you made that interpretation, then your parents behaviour made sense to you."

"Yes, said Sarah, I can see that."

"And, more importantly, from that day forward you believed it to be *the truth,* a fact in your world about you, that has never been challenged up until now?"

Step 4 – Interpret Alternatives

"I'm not good enough was just one logical interpretation or conclusion that you came to when you were very young. Let's see what other possible interpretations about your experiences as a child you can come up with, now you are an adult. Looking back to when you were just a kid with the exact same events and experiences, what other interpretations of your parents behaviour can you come up with now, that didn't occur to you at the time?"

Sarah thought long and hard....."How about this?"

- My parents were just busy with other things. It had nothing to do with me being good enough or not good enough.

- My parents were also brought up in similar situations and their actions were more to do with them than me.

- My parents just thought it was the right way to bring up kids, to let them get on with it, it had nothing to do with me being good enough or not.

- My parents were under pressure to pay a big mortgage and as a result there wasn't much time for me, but it didn't mean I wasn't loved or that I wasn't good enough.

- My parents were just acting out of their beliefs. They didn't want to praise me because they thought I might get a big head. It had nothing to do with me being good enough or not.

"Good stuff, I smiled. Can you see that each of these statements could explain your parents behaviour just as well as the conclusion that you reached as a kid, that you weren't good enough?"

"That's right, she replied, rubbing a small tear away as the realisation was beginning to dawn.

Step 5 – Events Have No Meaning

"If you go back in your mind Sarah, and picture yourself on the farm, looking back at all those events you described to me, didn't it seem like you can see **I'm not good enough** at those times? In all of those pictures in your mind you can see **I'm not good enough** as a fact to be seen in physical reality?"

"Yes it does." she replied.

"But can you actually *see* the belief as a physical thing? Something you can point to and touch and hold?"

Sarah hesitated for quite a while.

"No, I can't hold it and touch it."

"Interesting, I replied......... Why not?"

Sarah paused again, this time for much longer....

"Because it doesn't exist, she replied, keeping herself together. It was just something I made up at the time when I was young."

"So if **I'm not good enough** doesn't exist as a *fact* in the world and you can't touch it or hold it, where has it been all these years?"

"In my mind." Said Sarah.

"That's right, so what did you actually see for real?" I asked.

"I just saw my Dad not being around much. I just saw my parents behaviour. That's all I really saw for real."

"That's right, I replied. Even though **I'm not good enough** was never *the* truth, once you *made it* the truth, you continued to live your life as if it *were* the truth."

"In other words there is no meaning 'out there in the world' to be seen as a fact, until our minds give one to the events that happen."

"Yes, I can see that now, said Sarah."

"The reason why most people find it hard to totally eliminate a limiting belief is because they continue to integrate their belief with the thing that actually happened. Because the event or subsequent events did actually happen, they think they can 'see' their belief 'in' the event. In their minds they never realise that the belief they hold and the events that happened are two totally separate entities."

"Wow, that's incredible," Sarah replied, exhilarated.

"Once you make an interpretation about yourself, it becomes your truth. That belief becomes a core belief of your self-concept or the truth about you. It affects everything you do and say and affects what you will attract into your life. It becomes the filter or lens in which we view all situations, because you believe it *is* a fact in your world."

"Unbelievable," Sarah replied, stunned at her new awareness.

Step 6 – Feel It

"At the time when you were young it probably felt like you weren't good enough when Dad wasn't around much or you didn't get the attention you wanted right?" I asked.

"Yes, I did, that's true, it did feel like that."

"And the reason why you felt like that is because of the *meaning* you gave your parents behaviour or actions at the time. If you give your parents behaviour a different meaning, like one of the others that you came up with earlier, such as,

"My parents were just busy with other things and it had nothing to do with me being good enough, does the feeling change?"

"Yes it does, of course it does, said Sarah. It doesn't have any emotion in it at all..."

"Great, so can you now understand that it was the "meaning" you choose to give to your parents behaviour that caused you to feel, "I'm not good enough, not the actual behaviour of your parents?"

"Yes, I understand it fully now," said Sarah."

Step 7 – Say It

"Great, so right at the start of the process, about twenty minutes ago, you believed **I'm not good enough** to be the truth about you. Just look inside yourself now and ask yourself this - is **I'm not good enough** still the truth about you?"

"No, no it's not," said Sarah.

"Say the belief out loud just to make sure," I asked. I want to make sure it's definitely gone.

"I'm not good enough." Sarah replied.

"Has it gone? Is there ANY emotion in saying those words now, at all?

"Yes, it's gone! It's just flat when I say it. I realise now it was just something I made up as a kid thirty years ago. Wow! That's amazing."

"Ok Sarah, brilliant, well done! So, you eliminated that one belief. It will never come back and there is nothing more you have to do. Other techniques will have you repeat things over and over again, but with this process, you go through it once and you're done."

"However, having said that, we need to find *all* of the beliefs that underpin the complete pattern you described to me at the start-in this case, the fear of speaking in public. Once we identify *all* the beliefs and eliminate them, the fear will completely disappear."

"Once will identify all your unwanted patterns of behaviour, and eliminate all the beliefs that cause them, there will be no resistance to going out into the world and taking the actions necessary in order for you to get what you want. Does that make sense?"

"Totally," Sarah replied, "Let's get on with it!"

The Handbrake Effect

Eliminating your first belief is a huge breakthrough for most people, as it was for Sarah. Her entire life had been spent carrying around this limiting belief about herself that was never a fact. I call it the "Handbrake Effect." Have you ever driven your car with the brakes on? I can remember times when I've tried to nip out quickly at a busy roundabout and found that my car didn't have the same power that it usually has. I'd look down and realise the handbrake had been partly pulled on from the start of the entire journey. What a ridiculous way to drive a car!

Perhaps you've had the same experience? You pulled away from the curb in your car and as you did it felt a bit sluggish. It didn't have the pick-up you've come to expect. Even pushing harder on the accelerator didn't seem to help that much. And when you took your foot off the accelerator the car slowed down quickly. "Aha!" You reached down perhaps a little sheepishly and *fully* released the handbrake.

Remember how you felt as the brakes were released? As the power of the engine surged towards the wheels, how did you feel? Yes, the "Aha" moment will have been there, kind of like when you solve a puzzle, but there was also a kind of *relief* feeling - a sense of "that's more like it."

When it comes to success we think the answer is to mentally put a "bigger engine" in. What I mean by this is learn more stuff and gather more information. Most of us have enough information, the problem is we don't implement it to the degree that we could.

What you really have to do is release the beliefs that are causing you to "go slow" in the first place. When you get *both* aspects of your mind-power working for you, (the right power in *and* the handbrake released) then your productivity surges forward quickly and automatically *without* resistance.

> *"You'll see it when you believe it."*
> **– Dr Wayne Dyer**

We try to solve problems in our personal lives - as well as in business, with strategies that are consistent with the unconscious "self-concept" beliefs we have about ourselves in these areas. Because we think that we discovered our beliefs, "in the world" and have evidence for them, we strongly resist any strategies or ideas that are inconsistent with them. When we fully understand and realise that we never "saw in the world" what we believe, but we only interpreted it as such, the belief disappears for good and we are no longer crippled and held back by its power. We begin to be open to other possibilities that we just couldn't accept or see as possible for us, previous to the belief being eliminated. The great thing about this process is that it could be used to shift entire paradigms in business organisations as well as individual minds for performance.

Why Most Sales Training Doesn't Work

On any given day thousands of salespeople are being trained to be more effective. They are taught how to listen to their customers, how to handle objections, how to be more effective at cold calling, how to handle charging more money than competitors for similar products and services, and how to close. Some of these "skill" courses are effective. Unfortunately however, far too often the courses do not improve sales at all. Why not?

The answer is simple: ***Virtually none of these courses help the salespeople eliminate their existing beliefs that prevent them from being more effective in the first place.***

Let me give you a few examples.

No matter what skills or experience a salesperson might have, if he has the belief, ***What makes me good enough are my achievements***, his life will be run by what he is able to achieve and by showing others his achievements. Such a person is likely to be afraid to take on anything that he is not absolutely positive will result in an achievement he can shout about. Since sales calls usually have a significant amount of risk in them, someone with this belief might resist making certain sales calls.

No matter what skills or experience a salesperson might have, if he has the belief, ***The only way to make a sale is to have the lowest price***, he will resist selling a product that has a higher price even if it has more value than a competitor's. I have had many managers tell me that they hear the words of this belief from their salespeople frequently as an excuse for not making sales. When the managers provided their salespeople with a lot of information about the company's products and services and why they were worth much more than what their competitors were offering, their salespeople usually responded, "Yes, maybe so, but it's almost impossible to make a sale when we have a higher price."

No matter what skills or experience a salesperson might have, if he or she has a few negative self-concept beliefs, such as *I'm not good enough, I'm not capable or competent,* or *I'm powerless*, they will make him or her doubt their own ability and lower self-confidence. As a result the salesperson is unlikely to do all that he is potentially capable of. He is also likely to be perceived as unsure of himself by potential customers or clients.

No matter what skills or experience a salesperson might have, if he has the belief, *What makes me good enough is having people think well of me*, he will be afraid of rejection and will have a difficult time making cold calls. That belief leads to people being afraid to do anything that might result in people not thinking well of them and usually do only those things that people are sure to like. Whenever you call people you don't know, there is always the possibility the call might make them angry and they may hang up on you. For someone with this belief, this would be very scary.

No matter what skills or experience a salesperson might have, if he has the belief, *Mistakes and failure are bad*, he will be afraid to try anything new or different for fear of making a mistake or failing. If the tried and true are sufficient, salespeople with this belief might produce satisfactory results, but if innovative approaches to making sales are required, then this will be virtually impossible for a salesperson with this belief.

Personal and professional limiting beliefs can seriously sabotage salespeople in many other ways too. The moral of this story is, "In addition to providing skills training for your salespeople, make sure you also help them get rid of any limiting beliefs."

Try the process if you or the salespeople in your company are not using all the skills, tools and training they possess and seem to be stopping short of their full potential. You'll be amazed at how quickly eliminating a few beliefs can improve sales results-fast.

Getting Rid of the Belief, "I Can't …"

A while ago while in a business consulting session, it dawned on me that there was one massive crippling belief that was rampant in nearly every business I had ever worked in. And this belief was not only the most common belief in organisations, it was, in my opinion, the biggest single barrier that most people have as well.

What is this belief?…..*I can't*

"I can't find the right people." "I can't possibly find the time to do that." "We can't find the employees we need." "I can't get the help I need." "We can't possibly finish the project as quickly as the client wants." And the list goes on and on and on. If you work in a big company you probably hear, *I can't* … all day long. And if someone believes something "can't be done," then the chances are slim to nil that it *will* get done.

This belief, like any other belief is obviously very restricting and can be easily eliminated using the **SHIFT B.E.L.I.E.F.S System™**. We have used the process repeatedly in our organisational work for many years. (We have helped hundreds of businesses in the UK eliminate beliefs that kept the organisations from realising their full potential).

The only difficulty is that I couldn't be at every meeting, of every business, to hear each *'I can't'* being expressed and eliminate them. It currently takes time to train people to be effective with these processes. So I needed to teach a process that others could teach quickly, that could eliminate the innumerable *I can't* … beliefs.

When a belief is eliminated possibilities are created that didn't exist before (What can't be done is not a possibility). As soon as it *can* be done, a new possibility comes into existence for us. For example, if we can't raise the money we need, raising the money is not a possibility for us, so we don't bother trying. When the belief is eliminated, raising the money suddenly becomes a possibility.

This process can generally be taught to people in about forty minutes. I've taught it to hundreds of business owners, who then taught it to others in their own companies.

Because *I can't* ... shows up in our personal lives almost as often as in organisations, I thought I would explain in this section of the book how it all works. Here are the basic steps of the process so you can use it in your organisation or with friends and family.

Creating Possibilities

This is a modified belief process that is used to eliminate *I can't* ....beliefs, in order to enhance innovation and create new possibilities.

You will usually hear someone state, *I can't* .... out loud. If you are trying to help someone find their unconscious *I can't* ... beliefs, you can ask the following three questions:

1. What do you want to have happen?

2. What do you have to do to make this happen?

3. What's in the way of you doing that now?

(The answer will be, *I can't ... because* ....).

1. What is it you have to do or can't do? (NOTE: If someone states the belief in a positive way, for example, "we must," turn it into the negative version, "we can't."

2. How do you know that? What happened that led to the belief being formed? (The source here is not childhood, but one's recent experience).

3. Can you see that your belief made sense given your experience? (The answer will always be, yes).

4. You saw that it couldn't be done **the way** you did it, at **that** time, under **those** circumstances. Can you say with absolute certainty

that it could never be done **any** way under **any** circumstances in the future? (Logically, the answer will always have to be, no. You can never say anything about the future with absolute certainty).

5. Couldn't your past experience also mean: I haven't found a way to do it *yet*, but that does not mean that it can't be done? (Again, the answer will always be, yes).

6. Can you see that your belief (I can't) is only a description of the way it was in the past and not the truth about the future? (The answer will be, yes, which is acknowledging that the belief is no longer the truth).

7. If it's not the truth that *I can't ... (state the belief)*, how would you solve the problem if you could do it? (The *I can't ...* belief is gone after Step #6). If you are trying to solve a problem and someone stops the conversation with the belief, *We can't ...*after the belief is gone you can return to the discussion and now find a solution.

Try using the process in your business and then email me about your results at this address: simon@simonjgilbert.com

The Identity Thief

When we recognise that something we have held as a belief is in fact only one of many various alternative interpretations of what actually occurred (**EVENT**) and when we realise we never saw the belief in the world, and that events have no meaning until we give them one (**INTERPRETATION**) the belief disappears. There is big shift in identity, self-concept and awareness.

Clients often look and feel lighter when they permanently eliminate a belief but there is a much bigger behind the scenes cognitive process going on. Clients come to realise that their life up until this point, has been entirely consistent with the belief they have just eliminated- even though it never really was "the truth" about them. It's a much bigger deal than I can try and communicate to you in a book.

Richard, a financial advisor, went through the process with me and was very quick to catch on towards the end of the process. He realised that if when he was small he had the awareness to "chose" an interpretation that was empowering or at least not limiting in any way, then his life would have been consistent with that belief today. For example, if he had chosen, "My parents have unrealistic expectations of a kid my age," as an interpretation of certain events, instead of "Mistakes and failures are bad," which he did choose when he was younger, then his life would have been a perfect reflection of his parents having unrealistic expectations. This ingrained belief would have had an entirely different perspective on how the world appears to be. In other words, Richard really understood that he does create his beliefs and his beliefs determine his entire life.

This is very important for someone to understand. It is massively empowering for someone to understand that they really do create their own reality. It's common for a client to start challenging everything that doesn't serve them, simply because they start to get an awareness of who they really are. Interestingly, there are people who don't want to know this information, simply because it gives them an excuse to continue to blame everyone and everything "outside" of themselves. They don't want to take responsibility. Going through the process is not a witch hunt on your parents for being "bad parents" either. Ultimately it was your decision to choose whatever beliefs you have, even though you were only small. In my experience it's not because parents deliberately do or say things to upset their kids, most parents love their kids, it's just that they are ignorant to what their kids *might* conclude as a result of the things they do or say repeatedly.

It also doesn't matter whether you believe that your parents were amazing either. Often, some parents do everything for their children and never let them explore and get into things. They never let them out of their sight, only take them to "soft play" and never let them roll in the mud with the "rough kids." They effectively treat their kids like little princes or princesses. They believe that this is the way kids should be brought up so that nothing bad happens to them and to protect them from getting hurt. Kids like this often grow up with "no balls," with disempowering beliefs such as, "I'm powerless" or "I'm not capable." They don't get to choose to do what they really want to do. Life is continually dictated to them by their parents.

Having listened to a lot of top Entrepreneurs it becomes apparent that one of the most empowering things you can do is to teach your children that it's actually ok and natural to fail. Our kids are going to fail lots of times no matter what they do so why not just make it a part of the process of winning instead of protecting them from it?

Why not encourage them to get stuck in and make lots of mistakes?

"When I was growing up, my dad would encourage my brother and I to fail. We would be sitting at the dinner table and he would ask, 'So what did you guys fail at this week?' If we didn't have something to contribute, he would be disappointed. When I did fail at something, he'd high-five me. What I didn't realise at the time was that he was completely reframing my definition of failure at a young age. To me, failure means not trying; failure isn't the outcome. If I have to look at myself in the mirror and say, 'I didn't try that because I was scared,' that is failure." **– Sara Blakely – Founder of Spanx**

Once you have created a belief you have created a reality (for you at least) in which your belief is "the truth." Your life, as I said earlier becomes consistent with that belief. You have constant evidence flowing into your consciousness that the belief is "true." You have a hard time trying to imagine more empowering actions or behaviour because it is inconsistent with how you see yourself and your current beliefs. What happens is your behaviour continues to be consistent with your belief, even if it's sabotaging you or limiting you. "That's just the way it is" or "That's just the way I am" is a common phrase used by people who get fed up with trying to change their behaviour without changing the beliefs that cause behaviour. They become cynical, sceptical and disillusioned with their personal development and growth because, "nothing works."

Conventional Help

Most help that people get comes from trainers, coaches and others that assume that there is an objective world "out there" in which people are trying to deal with. Therefore the role of the facilitator is to make it easier for people to cope with this world "out there." The **SHIFT B.E.L.I.E.F.S System™** process on the other hand assumes that there is no reality independent of your beliefs. Therefore, altering your beliefs at the level of identity not only changes your behaviour, your feelings and how you perceive the world, it literally changes the world in which you live.

Because we create the world as we experience it, we can change it as fast as we like by changing beliefs at the level of identity. In other words your success will come as slow or as fast as you decide, depending on how many limiting beliefs you eliminate and the consequences of them. Your job now, if you fully understand the process, is to identify the beliefs holding you back from your personal path to riches and eliminate them all.

Expectation Theory

Expectation theory holds that your fundamental beliefs about yourself and your world are the principal determinants of your success in life. The practical understanding of this can be explained in the following statements.

- The beliefs you hold are the direct result of your interpretations of events you have engaged in.

- Your beliefs, in turn, create your expectations about results and future outcomes.

- Your expectations, in turn, determine your attitude.

- Your attitude determines your behaviour.

- Your behaviour and actions produces results.

So you can't change your results by changing your results. You have to change at the level of identity, because everything stems from there. Your beliefs about yourself represent decisions you have made in the past about yourself and what you expect or do not expect to accomplish in the future. These decisions are being repeated as you go through life.

They continuously control your thinking, direct your behaviour and determine your relative level of performance. How you perform in any area of your business or life is largely a function of your deep-seated beliefs.

Your mind is the dynamic force behind the marvellous success system within you. Whatever you believe, picture in your mind, and think about most of the time, you eventually bring into your reality. In its simplest form, expectation theory says that you generally get what you expect, not what you want or like. Wants are held in the conscious mind, but expectations are held in the subconscious, the power house of performance.

The breakthrough comes when you realise that your existing belief system that you now possess, can't possibly get you to where you really want to go. If it could, surely you would be there by now? If you had the right belief system in the first place, then chances are you would probably be where you wanted to be years ago. This really hacked me off when I finally understood it all, thinking of how many years I'd wasted, trying to understand why things weren't happening for me despite everything I'd tried.

But, it also excited me as well, as I had finally found the keys to the vault that I'd been looking for, for so long. I knew I had enough time to make amends. The point I'm trying to make is this;

The rewards that you and I receive in life do not come because of our potential. They come as a result of our performance.

Everything else is just bullshit. People pretending to be more successful than they really are (but not going anywhere) is caused by limiting beliefs. They are continually concerned by the opinions of others so they feel they have to pretend that they are something other than what and who they really are. The thing is, we don't really hide anything to the people around us because we can't sustain it.

Napoleon Hill, stated that one of the biggest fears in life was the "fear of criticism", second only to the fear of loss or poverty. The interesting thing about this, is that unless you are willing to eliminate your beliefs in order to stand out in life and take some flak, you will probably be at the mercy of the fear of criticism, (and subsequent mediocrity) all your life. In a crowded marketplace you have to stand out. This is a real problem for most people. They don't know who they really are and how to shield themselves from potential criticism and negativity.

Ask yourself this vital question: Do you have adequate knowledge of how your mind works? Do you understand the way you think and why you respond and behave the way you do? Do you truly understand the potential you possess? The average person doesn't. Many people like to read books that contain the potential for change and can appear knowledgeable on many related subjects. But unless you want to appear on TV's "Eggheads" who cares? Performance is everything. <u>Knowing and doing are poles apart.</u>

What's Really Holding You Back?

Joe had been seeing a doctor for three years for treatment of the fear that he had of monsters under his bed. It had been years since he had gotten a good night's sleep. Furthermore, his progress was very poor, and he knew it. So, one day he stops seeing his usual doctor and decides to try a totally different approach to his problem. A few weeks later, Joe's former doctor meets him in the supermarket, and is surprised to find him looking well-rested, energetic, and cheerful.

"Doc!" Joe says, "It's amazing! I'm cured!"

"That's great news!" the doc says. "You seem to be doing much better. How come?"

"I went to see someone else," Joe says enthusiastically, "And he cured me in just ONE session!"

"One?!" The doc asks incredulously.

"Yeah," continues Joe, "My new guy gets to the root of the problem quick."

"Really?" the doc asks. "How did he cure you in just one session?"

"Oh, easy," says Joe. "He just told me to cut the bloody legs off the bed......"

As you look at the world you may feel at times that it seems impossible to make changes quickly. The media deliberately feeds you stories that make you fearful in an attempt to keep you watching or listening. A belief is a feeling of being *sure* that something exists or that something is true.

We all have hundreds of different beliefs about ourselves and the world around us. Some are supportive and helpful, others are not. All of them however affect our life.

Beliefs are like inner rivers of the mind, some like gentle streams and others more like torrential rapids. If you look at your own life, you may have some problems that have bothered you for years. You might have tried all sorts of different programs, books, coaches or groups to help you because you really want to make things happen for you. Maybe you want to be a high achiever, a great leader, or perform to the best of your abilities. Chances are you keep slipping back into old and familiar patterns and you can't figure out why and what to do. Why can't you consistently achieve what you think you should be capable of achieving?

You are no doubt reading this book because you are a seeker and are committed to making changes, but you haven't yet been able to attain what you most passionately want. For you, you know there is a solution for you.....somewhere.

Are You Limited by Your Beliefs?

What do you really mean when you say you *believe* something? A belief is a statement about reality that you think is "the truth." This belief shapes your behaviour, your emotions, attitudes, expectations, actions and the results you get. Each of your beliefs serves as a box that defines limits and controls your behaviour and performance.

As you've seen, your core beliefs were formed before the age of six in early childhood. These are the beliefs that shape who you are and are extremely influential in determining how you see yourself and how you deal with the world "out there."

Many medical experts, performance psychologists and other experts agree that possessing self-esteem within a positive self-concept is the key to living as empowered adults. In my own experience, after having spoken with thousands of people, I found that limiting beliefs were the root of almost every undesirable pattern of behaviour that people presented.

"People think I am confident because I can address a room full of people. The reality is that I spend most of my time thinking that I'm not good enough. If I give a speech, I spend the next few days thinking about all the mistakes I made, rather than the difference I made. This has severely limited my business and personal growth. It has kept me in a place of low confidence, so that I'm less willing to take on more challenging work." - David Allen

David, a top executive in his company, spent an hour of our first session together describing how many businesses were often trying to head hunt him as CEO, how wealthy he was, and how many business successes he had. But as we worked together, David discovered something that truly astonished him. First he discovered the belief, **I'm not good enough** which was his interpretation of why he had received very little attention from his parents (His father used to work away in the Middle East for months at a time). He then remembered that when he was little, his parents only used to give him positive attention when he exceeded their expectations. He also formed the belief, **What makes me good enough is exceeding people's expectations.** He grew into a driven businessman, accumulating wealth and success along the way, but he never really felt that he had done enough. His belief kept him extremely busy, productive and full on, but there was little satisfaction from his work, and life was just passing him by without any happiness or real joy.

Whilst others may have looked at David's achievements and hailed him as a resounding success with very high self-esteem, the reality was he never really felt good about himself. Having a high self-concept of yourself is not about conceit, bragging, or acting important. Nor is it trying to convince others you are important. We are not talking "fake it till you make it," what we are talking about is having a high positive self-concept because you *know* that no matter what happens, you can handle it and you are ok just the way you are. In David's case, once we had eliminated these beliefs and others, the drive was still there to get things done, but the stress and anxiety of having to prove himself to others was gone forever. Many people like David retire and totally lose the perceived prestige that comes with a high powered job or position. They lose their identity because over the years they have built their entire persona around working, accumulating and "putting in the hours."

Most People Agree….and They Are Wrong

Because I'm in the business of getting results quickly, I'm frequently telling people that changing is pretty easy if you've got the formula and you know how to do it. Almost without exception, I am greeted with a face of bewilderment and a raised eye of suspicion!

"Oh Yeah, I'm sure it is, what do you mean it's easy?, I've been trying for years!" The most ironic thing about the work I do, is that most people don't think something *could* be easy and quick to change because they have the belief, **Change is hard and takes a long time** or at least some variation of this belief. The very belief that is holding them back from the success they want is causing them to be sceptical in the first place! Part of the reason for writing this book is so that you can hopefully understand that it doesn't have to be hard *unless you choose* it to be.

Despite this conventional thinking people don't really resist change, they resist *being* changed. Nobody wants to be forced to change, but if they make the decision, then that's ok.

What appears to be resistance to change is nothing more than people acting consistently with their beliefs. When people change their beliefs, change occurs naturally and effortlessly.

> "If I'm being honest, I was extremely sceptical at first, but in just fifteen minutes Simon eliminated a limiting belief that had been unconsciously holding me back for forty-two years. Once I'd seen the process work for me once, I was chomping at the bit to 'empty the mental dustbin' of all the other crap in there."
> – Mike Kennedy

Most self-help stuff tries to help you cope better with the world. The **SHIFT B.E.L.I.E.F.S System™** enables you to *change* your world (which you created in the first place!) by permanently eliminating beliefs about who you think you are, and by understanding that you are also creating your feelings moment by moment, based on whatever interpretation you are giving your external events.

Pike Syndrome

Let me tell you about an experiment. An experiment with a pike to be precise.

The pike. A rather scary looking fish. An effective hunter and a force to be reckoned with... if you're a small fish that is.

More than a century ago, German zoologist Karl Möbius conducted an interesting experiment. He placed an unsuspecting pike in a glass tank filled with water. He then divided the tank into two parts, by placing a glass panel in the middle of the tank. There upon the curious biologist placed some smaller fish in the tank. The pike probably thought it was its birthday! What the poor pike didn't notice however, was the glass barrier in between its own part of the tank and the side filled with the juicy prey.

Every time the pike would launch itself at a tasty little fish, it would painfully crash into the barrier. The pike would keep trying and kept having painful encounters with the glass barrier. After many failed attempts (and presumably with a very sore nose) the pike ceased its attacks. It had 'learned' attacking the small fish was futile. Worse, it now associated attacking the little fishes with pain.

After some time, Möbius pulled out the barrier. Although there now was nothing left to stop the pike from filling its belly, it would keep ignoring the frolicking fish-even when they swam right up to its nose. Although the reason to remain inactive was gone, the predatory fish kept acting on it, or rather *not* acting on it....

Möbius had mercy on the pike and fed it. Other researchers that later repeated the experiment were less lenient though. They often stood by while the once mighty predator **starved to death**...

Nature teaches us a valuable lesson here. Many businesses are making the same mistake the poor pike made. Of the many habits and procedures we get involved in on a day-to-day basis we have long forgotten *why* they became a habit in the first place. It's a good idea to question fixed beliefs and 'obvious' ways to deal with a familiar situation.

Entrepreneurs especially should regularly ask themselves "Do I suffer from the Pike syndrome?" Ask yourself, "Why do I always act this way?" and "Are the reasons why I started doing this still valid?"

You might not be very interested in biology, but surely you recognise the lesson here. Are you displaying 'pike behaviour?' Are you pikey? Or do you know people who are acting dangerously pike-like? I'm sure you do...

How Do Your Beliefs Affect You?

"The beliefs that we hold in our mind create the biology and behaviour of our lives" – Dr Bruce Lipton

Beliefs are not just abstract things that have an impact on your psychology, they exist in the form of thought patterns that exist in your neurology and physical body. They are very real electrochemical signals that are broadcast throughout your entire body. Thoughts are things. Beliefs are the content and substance of those thoughts. To really change your life, change your beliefs first and your thoughts will automatically follow.

Your beliefs not only dictate your attitude to life but also affect your physical body depending upon whether your beliefs are helpful to you or not. Let's take a look at a very real example.

Suppose you have an important sales meeting with a prospective client or customer.

You are new to the industry, but you fully believe in your product, your abilities and your company to deliver the goods at a competitive price. Your positive attitude is also fuelled by the belief that you have a very high conversion rate based on previous selling experiences although in a different industry. As you arrive at the doors of the clients plush London offices, your beliefs set up a very real cascade of physical events: they stimulate positive, life enhancing chemicals to flow through your brain and nervous system, which in turn helps you to up your performance levels. The result is that you feel less stressed than many others would feel and you are able to relax with your presentation. This relaxed body gives off an unconscious vibration of energy to whoever is in near proximity. It helps you to think more clearly and to speak with authority and competence. Almost everything that occurs at the presentation will have started as a chain of events fuelled by your beliefs.

Now let's change only *two* aspects of the same situation above. Keeping everything the same, same product, same company representation that can deliver at a competitive price and same experience level in the industry. However this time the exception is that the salesperson has two unconscious beliefs.

1. **I'm not worthy**

2. **I'm not capable**

This time, on arrival at the plush London office your attitude is not so positive. You see the beautifully polished Aston Martin parked in the "Director's Only" parking space, the marble floors and the comings and goings of people in a hurry. You start to doubt your worthiness benchmarked against such opulence. Maybe you start to reconsider your decision to sell to high end clients. Maybe your self-concept screams out, "Oi, Faker! Get back flogging floor paint on the Industrial Estate's where you belong!" Suddenly your dreams of becoming the next "Wolf of Wall Street", more likely limp into the reality of the "Mouse from Middlesbrough." Your whole physical vibration changes and you get a tightness in your upper torso reflecting these unwanted beliefs. Even if you manage to splutter out a half decent presentation, you don't ask for the business because there's no point, you know they are only humouring you to fill in the 20 minutes you said it would take to see them. You couldn't stand the humility of rejection so rather than ask for the order you pack up, "let them think about it" and politely leave. Notice however that the game was over *before* you even stepped through the door.

If, in your overall belief system your world is a hard place and success is difficult, you will have to constantly prove your worth and abilities time and time again. When it comes to selling, your thoughts will be stimulating a surge of chemicals that put your body into a major stress response.

Adrenalin can up your performance making you sharp and focused, but when it rides on the back of self-limiting beliefs, it can make you appear less articulate and cause you to stumble over your words and appear timid.

We all know people who may not be especially talented or qualified, but are stellar at promoting themselves and often win opportunities that we thought should have gone elsewhere. Are they just lucky or good bull-shitters? What do they have that works so well to their advantage? The answer is pretty simple. It's the positive, unconscious beliefs they have about themselves and their world. All those characteristics we associate with a person's personality are really the beliefs, self-image and self-concept bursting through to the surface of their consciousness. If you want to know what your beliefs are in any area of your life all you need to do is take a good look at your results in that area. It really is that simple.

Why People Don't Ask for Help

I don't know the answer for sure, but here are some possibilities:

- They believe that permanent change is impossible.

- They feel that change might be possible for others but not for themselves.

- They are convinced that living with an unpleasant situation is an unavoidable part of being human.

- They've given up any hope of permanent improvement after so many disappointments.

- They are embarrassed about having any negative beliefs and won't ask for help.

It's understandable why so many people have reached most of these conclusions. They have tried very hard to improve their lives for many years without success. I think being embarrassed is a real issue, especially for men. The idea of admitting to being less than bulletproof isn't exactly appealing! However, I figured that if I could explain *why* we have the limiting beliefs we hold today-that it was an almost unavoidable conclusion of growing up for everyone, then it would hopefully make it more acceptable to ask for help in eliminating these beliefs. I rather hope that people will recognise it's totally possible to eliminate limiting beliefs for good, and maybe suffer a temporary embarrassment, than hold a lifelong feeling of fear, inadequacy and limitation.

I've Experienced the Same Frustration

I know this frustration first hand. In the past I always knew it was my beliefs that were holding me back. I'd tried lots of so called belief elimination programs, group workshops, Cd's, and a whole lot of books and yet I saw very little improvement in my results. In spite of all this I never gave up even after decades of frustration and despair. I knew there had to be an answer and eventually I would find it. Deep down I knew that for every problem there has to be a solution.

Ultimately, I had to bring all of the pieces of this "mind puzzle" together, through twenty-five years of arduous research, in order to get a complete solution to permanent behavioural change and personal performance.

The Answers Within

As I've explained earlier, almost all of our behavioural problems are the result of our perceptions of reality, not reality itself. Our perceptions being the result of our beliefs about ourselves and reality, and the meaning we give moment-to-moment events. Thus, almost all of our problems are self-imposed-and that's good news. If we are the source of our problems, that means we have the ability to eliminate them for good. Right now you're starting to understand how you were programmed from a very early age. Let's now take a look at how our beliefs affect us today in two of the most important areas of being an Entrepreneur. Money and success.....

EXERCISES

What Behavioural or Emotional Pattern do you want to eliminate?

_____

_____

_____

_____

What beliefs are responsible for this?

_____

_____

_____

_____

Why doesn't most training work as effectively as it should?

_____

_____

_____

_____

What is your biggest "I Can't" standing in the way?

_____

_____

_____

_____

Chapter 5

Money, Success and You

There is a powerful and persistent concept running right through the core of this book. It's not really a new idea, and nor did I invent it, but this entire book is aimed at helping you accept it and believe it.

It is a basic truth, proven time and time again by people in all walks of life. It really hit home with me after reading Napoleon Hill's great book, "Think and Grow Rich." I often run mastermind groups on Hill's work and in preparing for the groups I must have read it at least a hundred times! In fact, I still read it today and every time I do I still learn something, but at a much deeper level. The one key idea that I want to share with you now is written in the very first few pages of the book before the introduction on "Mind Power."

"Success come to those who become SUCCESS CONSCIOUS. Failure comes to those who indifferently allow themselves to become FAILURE CONSCIOUS."

The truth is I must have read these lines probably like most people with the attitude of, "Yeah, that's a nice little quote, but what do I have to do to make it happen!" I was literally rejecting one of the fundamental basics of Hills philosophy as inconsequential. Then one day I heard a quote that went,

"If you read a good book through the second time, you won't see something in it that you didn't see before, you'll see something in your-self that wasn't there before."

I'm not sure as to which reading of the book caused me to stop and really understand the gravity of the lines mentioned, but it has now become my philosophy for nearly everything I do. Am I thinking about what I want or not? It's so simple, and because of its simplicity I think that's why I continued to miss the deep significance of it. I mentioned in the introduction of this book that at the core of Hill's philosophy was just four things:

- Desire - A clear vision of what you want.

- The belief that you will get it.

- A plan to put that belief into action.

- Persistence.

This then provides the basis for Hill's most famous quote:

"Anything the mind of man can conceive and believe it will achieve."

The reason I entitled this chapter, Money, Success and You, is because I want to get the point across that if you don't have a clear image in your mind of what prosperity is and what it means to you, it's virtually impossible for your mind to navigate towards it. So here's the deal. You may want to be a top performer and increase your income, but answer the following truthfully;

- Do I have a clear vision or goal of what I want? **Yes/No**

- Do I *really* believe I can get it? **Yes/No**

- Do I have a plan for getting what I want? **Yes/No**

If you answered yes to all three and are taking steps everyday towards your goal, well done you, it's only a matter of time before you get it. If one or more is missing from your success equation then take the time to sit down and do the work. It won't actually take that long. I'm not going to go into goals in this chapter as I covered this in my previous book, *"How Big Is Your But!"* so if you want a great goal setting and more importantly, goal achieving process, then take a look in there.

I'm going to assume you do know what you want. I'm not really interested in your particular goal for the time being, what I'm really interested in is *do you believe it?* Do you sincerely believe that you can have *anything* you want or not? If it's money you want, what do you *really* believe you have to do to get it?

This I find, is the real stumbling block for most people. Most people I speak to say they are on their way to success because they have a vision board of all their goals or because they've watched the movie, "The Secret" ten times, but there is no real belief in their voice. There's no real commitment, no fire in the belly, no balls.

Show Me the Money

Most people believe it's really hard to make a lot of money and yet some people think it's really easy to make a lot of money. So, which one is right? Both! We'll that can't be right you say, one has to be right the other has to be wrong! No, not at all, it's just a choice, but whatever you believe to be true is YOUR truth, nobody else's truth necessarily.

I think because most people don't understand the simple equation that links value to money, most people don't think they could possibly be worth a lot of money. In business, you and I are paid in the marketplace by the value we bring and how many lives we impact. To make a lot of money, we need to help a lot of people with a lot of value. To stay poor is to help only a small amount of people with very little value!

Many people say, Oh, I just couldn't be a millionaire, it's too much hassle. I think they say that because many entrepreneurs only see a duplication of what they are *already* thinking and doing in business as their only route to wealth.

Decision

Once you decide that you are going to create your own economy and become as wealthy as you want to be, you have made a commitment. Every decision is a commitment. I'm not talking about wishing and hoping; I'm talking about decisions which are active moves you make in the direction of your financial freedom. Decision is the beginning of action. At the very core of your consciousness are decisions residing: Healthy v Unhealthy, Happy v Unhappy or to be Rich or Poor. In fact, just put your hands out in front of you right now, about eighteen inches away, palms towards you and look carefully at both hands. Imagine in your left hand are images of struggle, boredom and mediocrity. In your right hand are images of fun, freedom and riches. Look at both of them for five seconds, back and forth and then choose the sodding right hand!

You see by default, if you're not choosing the right hand, the rich hand, then by mental law, you must be *choosing* the left! Here's some more,

- The choice to moan or do.

- The choice to blow money or invest it.

- The choice to lie or be honest (especially to yourself).

- The choice to drive drunk or sober.

- The choice to watch crap on TV or read a book that could help you move ahead.

- The choice to watch sport or play it.

- The choice to listen to the media or create your own economy.

- The choice to buy stuff to impress your friends or get new friends.

- The choice to get married after four weeks or not.

- The choice to spend £20,000 on a brand new car and it be worth £8500 in three years-time or invest that £20,000 into something that gives you a return.

- The choice to keep going or pack in.

- The choice to learn and grow or not learn and stay stuck.

Your choices spark the fires of future circumstances. The fabric of your life is sewn by the past and ongoing cumulative consequences of your choices, millions of them that you set in motion. If your dissatisfied with any aspect of your life, choose to do something different. "I am responsible for everything that happens to me" is a very powerful affirmation.

The reason why most people have been "unconsciously" choosing the left hand of mediocrity is because of all the negative information that has been bombarding their consciousness. To quote Napoleon Hill, they have "allowed" themselves to become failure conscious. This must be overcome before you can move forward. This mind-sweeping operation is crucial to developing prosperity consciousness.

 You may already be excited about your potential prosperity and you may already believe you want to be rich and can be rich, but I don't think that's enough until you can accept it at a deep emotional level of consciousness. The reason why most books on positive life changes haven't worked for most people who've read them is simply because they have overlooked the limiting beliefs and not offered techniques to permanently eliminate them. Until you identify and confront these emotional beliefs, you won't be free to achieve and enjoy the life you deserve.

Tipping the scale

Prosperity consciousness is a very *positive* belief system. Poverty consciousness is a very *negative* belief system. At any moment you can only have one dominating idea. When you have two conflicting beliefs the subconscious mind accepts the dominant belief. Since your poverty consciousness is likely to have been fed more and got a firmer foothold than your prosperity consciousness, it will tend to dominate you unless you put up a fight for control of your own mind.

Out of the night that covers me,
Black as the pit from pole to pole,
I thank whatever gods may be
For my unconquerable soul.

In the fell clutch of circumstance
I have not winced nor cried aloud.
Under the bludgeoning's of chance
My head is bloody, but unbowed.

Beyond this place of wrath and tears
Looms but the Horror of the shade,
And yet the menace of the years
Finds and shall find me unafraid.

It matters not how strait the gate,
How charged with punishments the scroll,
I am the master of my fate,
I am the captain of my soul.

– *William Ernest Henley* *(English poet)*

You must remove as much negative programming with respect to money, from your subconscious as you possibly can, to give yourself a fighting chance and tip the scales of fortune in your favour. In Chapter 4, **The SHIFT B.E.L.I.E.F.S System™** you have the system to help you do it. Bob Proctor, author of *"You Were Born Rich"* teaches that you must hold on to your image of prosperity no matter what your outside circumstances may be indicating. That's hard enough as it is, without getting bombarded by your own belief system as well. Do you see why most people don't take control of their mind? It's because they not only have to deal with the external physical world bombarding them with negative information, but they also have to deal with their own internal beliefs systems as well! What chance do you really stand, especially when you don't know this information?

The Goldilocks Effect

Goldilocks and the Three Bears is one of the most popular fairy tales in our English language. It is often used as a bedtime story to teach young kids that trespassing is fair game and it's ok to nick stuff that doesn't belong to you (just joking!).This common fable involves Goldilocks trying three of everything until it is just right. Her actions foster her perfectionism; after all, you would think Goldilocks would be satisfied with the first taste of porridge, it's not even her house! Readers of the fairy tale are often relieved to discover that after she gets rumbled by the three bears (whilst mistaking their bedroom for the local DFS bed trying-station), Goldilocks makes a quick escape out of the window, runs back into the forest, and saves herself from what could have otherwise been a devastating eighteen month suspended sentence……

Getting back to perfectionism, people who try to be perfect never really produce creative and valuable ideas. Perfectionism is a refusal to let yourself move ahead. It is a loop — an obsessive, debilitating closed system that causes you to get stuck in the details of what you are doing and makes you lose sight of the whole. Psychologists have long recognised the perfectionist complex as one of the most destructive to human growth and development. In terms of financial success, many people use perfectionism as an excuse. Waiting for perfection in any area of your life will usually guarantee permanent stalling in that area. Many people manifest their perfection complex by making "If only" excuses about their lack of prosperity.

If only I wasn't in debt….

If only I could just find my niche….

If only I could just find the right people….

If only I had more money….

If only it was easier…..

It isn't the man or woman who has it perfect who succeeds. People who have had all or most of the problems listed above have still made it. People who make money often make mistakes, and even have major setbacks, but they still believe they will eventually win.

There was a time when I really fancied myself as a bit of an art trader. In particular, contemporary art of which I had built up quite a good collection of limited edition prints. One day whilst running a small cleaning business I unfortunately damaged my back quite badly and I wasn't able to do any physical work.

The doctor told me I would have to be off work for at least six weeks. Jeez. Well, there was no way I was just going to just sit at home feeling sorry for myself without earning any money, so I turned to the internet for inspiration. After poking around for a while I got the idea that I would import some original artwork (of a Middlesbrough born artist!) from San Francisco. The English pound was strong against the American dollar and demand was high for the art. Armed with my credit card, I bought my first original piece at a cost of around £8500. Ten days later it arrived in a big wooden crate outside my tiny little cottage. I admired it for a while and secretly wished I could keep it. But that wasn't the plan. I put it back up for sale on the internet and was quickly offered £10,000 for it from a buyer in Birmingham.

"Get in there!" I shouted, as I put the phone down to the prospective buyer. He loved the piece and we made arrangements for him to turn up the following Saturday and hand over the cash.

Twenty minutes later, after I'd done the deal, I received an email from the gallery owner in San Francisco making me aware that the collection was moving on from her gallery and she would no longer be able to sell me anymore pictures after they had left her premises.

"I'll have two more," I replied confidently, knowing I'd already sold the first one for a healthy £1500 profit. I was on a roll. With another two originals on their way, I had now invested a total of £18,256 in original paintings. All on credit cards. Then my worst nightmare happened. The guy from Birmingham stopped answering his phone. When I eventually got hold of him he made a whole pile of excuses, but had simply got cold feet and changed his mind. So here I was sitting on over £18,000 worth of art that I'd paid retail for, hoping like hell I could sell it to someone else. After months of trying my best to sell them and pay off the credit cards, I had to admit temporary defeat. I offloaded them at a local auction house and made a loss of around £7,000. So, why do I tell you this story? Because of all the lessons that are woven within it. If I hadn't had lost that money when I first started, If I hadn't have got in the game, there would have been no lessons learned and it wouldn't have led me to what I do today.

The debt that was still on my credit card forced me to use my mind in ways I'd never done before. It made me come up with a plan of how to pay it off quickly. I had just re-read "Think and Grow Rich" and decided to use Carnegie's formula written in the book. I had to come up with a plan that would raise £10,000, in just one month. The book explains that you will receive a plan using the most appropriate methods available to you, based on your circumstances, provided you hold the image of what you want long enough and with emotion.

This I know is the key.

I wrote on a card that I would have in my possession £10,000 within one month. As I sat reading the card again and again, all of a sudden an idea popped into my mind that I could franchise my cleaning business, by selling off a part of a rather large geographical area that I controlled. I immediately got myself into action. I drafted up some franchisee agreements, created an operations manual and quickly put an advert in the local paper advertising the opportunity to do what I was doing (The offer was that good, I almost bought it back myself!). That same week I had four people interested in becoming a franchisee. Three weeks from getting the idea, I attracted the right person. After explaining the opportunity he gave me a physical cheque in my hand for £9995, plus £100 a month passive income for the next three years.

Had I not made the "mistake" with the artwork, I'm not sure whether I would have forced my mind to think in much bigger and smarter ways. I proved the concepts worked for myself, and continue to use them to this day. Desperation was a powerful motivator!

I Can't Afford It!

"I can't afford it" is probably the most overused statement of poverty conscious people. If you notice, when people respond with this statement there is no gap between the questioned being asked and the reply given – it's just an automatic response.

"We're going out in London next weekend, It's gonna be great! Do you want a come?"

"No, I can't afford it."

"I've got tickets for the show, do you fancy it?"

"Sorry, I can't afford it."

"We're going to Carluccio's restaurant at the weekend, would you like to join us?"

"Aww, I would do, but I can't afford it."

These people never give it one second of thought as to HOW they could do what they really want to do. It's conditioned behaviour, it's a habit and because they've done it for so long they don't even know it. They are imprisoned by an invisible force that is dictating a reality they don't even like.

No one's poverty consciousness was ever sorted with a bag full of money. It's an inside job. It's a state of mind that's emotionally charged and each person has to claim it for themselves.

Poverty consciousness is what we get by sabotaging ourselves. There's a part of you we could call the "inner pauper," that will always come up with excuses, indecisions, and limiting expectations of success. The inner pauper is always motivated by fear. Fear of failure, fear of never making it and then fear of losing it. Fear causes us to close our minds tightly against a much bigger prosperous idea. Confidence allows us to open our minds wide, letting fresh ideas in.

Years ago, whilst running a group mastermind, one of the participants was a guy called John who had just sold his printing business. He was still in a bit of a hole financially so was looking for a way out. I was discussing with the group the importance of holding onto the image of what we want, despite all outside evidence to the contrary.

"How am I supposed to hold on to the image of prosperity when I can't even pay my bills?" said John.

"Well, I replied, You've tried it one way, which is to focus on what's happening and how bad it is, and that has kept you mired in the problem. You know whatever you focus on you attract, based on the dominant thought principle, so continually focusing on how bad things are probably isn't going to work out for you in the future either is it? How can focusing on lack and limitation possibly work out for you when you say you want success and prosperity?" Answer? It can't.

I'm not one to baby people, I'd rather piss someone off and have them improve their results than agree with them when they start whinging. It's not that I'm heartless, far from it. It's just that some people need to stop blaming others and take responsibility before it's too late.

It wasn't really John's fault, that he couldn't accept the idea of prosperity. It's not really *anybody's* fault that we have the programming we have, but it's definitely our responsibility to change it. And change it fast.

Money Doesn't Grow On Trees

What this statement has to do with any real-life situation escapes me now, just as it did when I was a kid. I know money doesn't grow on trees. I also knew that my parents, though of modest means, could afford a couple of quid for us to go to the cinema as rare as it was. It's like saying you can't drive around town on a hoover. It doesn't really make any sense. However, we all know the message it's trying to deliver; *Money is in short supply and difficult to get.*

Not surprisingly, what your parents felt about money and what you should do with it, is the biggest indicator of where you are likely to have got your money consciousness from. I think parents who deliberately hide financial information from their kids contribute to a poverty consciousness for sure. Some parents have a lack of trust of each other and their children. Big in the news recently is whether you have a secret stash hidden from your partner. Nearly one in seven (13%) married UK adults has admitted to a secret 'stash of cash' which their partner doesn't know about, while a further 15% have had one in the past.

While most people (41%) cited 'financial independence' as the reason for keeping their money separate, 38% of people were worried their partner would want to spend the money, and one in five (20%) wanted to be sure their partner didn't just like them for their money.

Often parents hold back money from their kids with the justification of, "It'll all be yours one day," whilst secretly worrying that if they give some away, they are going to be left short. Even though I am well aware of the emotional fears and negative programming that lead to such actions on behalf of the parents, I still find it demoralising that so many parents seem to prefer that their children should enjoy their money after they die, rather than sharing that joy whilst they are alive.

I think it's important to state here that you can never change your parents poverty consciousness. You can only change your own.

It's a sad but well known psychological fact that some people fail deliberately just to "get even" with their parents in an on-going attempt to blame them for the situations they find themselves in. Unfortunately, what these people don't realise is that by putting negative energy into these situations only produces self-defeat. This is also true when you envy someone else who has achieved success. Some people looks at others achievements as a form of punishment, as if that persons success was rubbing their noses in it, whilst others view it as an opportunity to learn and grow.

It all boils down to interpretation.

Can Beliefs Keep You from Becoming Wealthy?

A few months ago I asked people on our database which beliefs they thought were keeping them from becoming wealthy. The top five were:

- You have to work hard to make money.

- I'm not deserving.

- I'll never have enough money.

- Money is a struggle.

- Life is difficult.

If you have any doubt about the impact of beliefs on your ability to earn and retain money, ask yourself this question: Imagine someone having these five beliefs. Then ask yourself: Do you think such a person is likely to be wealthy? … Do you think Alan Sugar, Richard Branson, or any other really wealthy person has these beliefs? You've gotta be kidding me!

Here's another way to demonstrate the power of beliefs to interfere with your ability to make money and accumulate wealth. Think back to the last book you read or the last workshop you took that told you exactly what you needed to do to make huge sums of money. You learned what actions you needed to take, didn't you? Now answer this question: Did you *do* what you learned to do, on a consistent basis?

For most people the answer is a resounding, "NO!"

In fact, as amazing as it might seem, people who sell courses that promise to help you make money report that many of the courses that are purchased at workshops are never even actually opened when the buyers get them home. Moreover, the free email support that accompanies many of these courses is rarely used.

The only way to make sense of these astonishing facts is to remember that knowing what to do is useless if you have beliefs in the way of acting on that knowledge.

- If you believe **you have to work hard to make money**, it just might not be worth the effort.

- If you believe **you aren't a deserving person**, you would likely sabotage any effort you make to become financially successful.

- If you believe **I'll never have enough money**, then what's the point of trying?

- If you believe **money is a struggle**, your life becomes a self-fulfilling prophecy.

- And if you believe **life is difficult**, then you will create a life that is difficult in most respects, including a lack of money.

There are tens of millions of people who are interested in self-improvement but generally there is two different but related focuses: financial success and personal growth.

People who primarily are interested in financial success seek out products that promise to help them make more money and end up with more wealth. People who primarily are interested in personal growth usually want to change their behaviour, such as stopping procrastination and their emotions of fear.

So although sometimes there is an overlap between these two groups, people tend to have one focus or the other.

Even for the people who do pursue both goals, I'm not sure that many people interested in self-improvement are aware that there is an inextricable connection between these two areas of life.

Although financial success can be affected by many different factors—including what product or service you are offering, the quality of the offering, to what market, competition, at what price, etc—one of the most critical factors that is often ignored but significantly affects your financial success is your mental and emotional state.

Whether the source of dysfunctional behaviour and emotions are beliefs or anything else, the chance of achieving and enjoying financial success in today's world is slim unless you are able to get rid of your dysfunctional behaviour and emotions. Let me explain why.

For many years, success in business depended on showing up every day and doing what you were told. If you did it well enough for long enough, you'd usually move up through the organisation you worked for and end up with a nice fat pension.

Financial success requires personal growth.

Today, showing up and doing the "right" thing is no longer enough, whether you work for yourself or someone else. More and more organisations are looking for creative, innovative, imaginative people who will figure out for themselves what needs to be done instead of just waiting to be told. If you do work for yourself then merely doing what many others do, the way *they* do it, is unlikely to provide you with significant financial success.

If that is what financial success requires in today's fast-changing world—where what worked yesterday is probably not going to work today, and certainly won't be what works tomorrow—then your behaviour and emotional state are going to be crucial.

Beliefs that Hinder Financial Success

What is the chance of you being innovative, taking chances and doing what makes sense to you (whether others approve or not) if you have even a few limiting beliefs?

In addition to the beliefs, what if also you have been conditioned to feel fear if you are rejected, if you are criticised or judged, or if you don't live up to the expectations of others?

People with beliefs and conditionings like these will have a hard time doing what they need to do to achieve financial success. Yes, they can learn what to do from a lot of great books and courses, but it will still be difficult to implement that really useful advice.

Double Money

I had a client called Peter who had eliminated a few negative self-concept beliefs and other negative beliefs about achieving financial success. One day I got a call from Peter, as he wanted to share some exciting news with me. Peter was a business consultant and so he had the capacity to turn things around pretty quickly. He told me that over the last couple of days he had informed his clients that his fee was going to double as of next month. *"All but one accepted the new rate,"* he told me, *"however, the majority said I should have done it years ago........I've just gone and bought myself a new Mercedes!"*

At that point I pulled out Peter's file and read some of the beliefs he had eliminated previously to raising his prices: **I'm not deserving, Money is hard to get, I'll never get what I want, and I'm not important.**

I then asked him, "Do you think you would have asked for the fee increase and bought the car of your dreams if you still had the beliefs you eliminated?" The stunned silence at the other end of the phone answered my question.

Obviously, *only* getting rid of limiting beliefs and conditionings is not guaranteed to insure financial abundance. You have to take action on your ideas as well. But the ability to take the type of actions required for financial success in today's world requires the ability to not be stopped by your fear of making mistakes, by what you think others may think of your behaviour, or by a lack of confidence.

So if financial success is your focus—and there is nothing wrong with that focus—make sure you handle your beliefs first. It will give you a much better chance of achieving financial success and it will certainly enable you to enjoy it more as well.

Prosperity Can Elude You For Many Reasons

Prosperity can also elude you because you don't ask for the money you deserve or do what you know you should do to earn it. Limiting beliefs cause these inappropriate behaviours as well.

In order to insure financial success, it would be useful to have, in additional to the absence of limiting money beliefs, a positive attitude about earning and having money, an effective strategy for getting it, and then the commitment to fully implement your strategy on a daily basis. You have to have a purpose.

If Money is Your Problem, Money is Not the Problem

Yes that's right, I haven't made a mistake in the subheading! Earning money is all about satisfying the wants and needs of others. But boy, did I take a long time to figure out this basic principal! I used to think how can I make more money, how can I get more money? As soon as I started to take the focus off me and found solutions to help other people, it was like I'd been walking around in the dark and someone had just handed me a million-candle-power torch! Nothing is bought, sold or traded that doesn't satisfy a need or fulfil someone's desire. Finding better and quicker ways to help serve your customers, colleagues, friends, family and others will lead you to the wealth you desire. I've found that when your thoughts concentrate on just yourself and *your* problems, you keep slipping back into a negative habit pattern.

Remember: Your problems are of no interest to the vast majority of people in your life; however, you can solve your own problems by helping others solve theirs.

Getting in the Success Zone

Ninety-seven percent of our population in the UK are quick to agree that success in life is a puzzle. It seems to be a perpetual struggle to figure out where all the pieces fit in order to make things happen. Every time we have the image coming together smoothly we sometime find ourselves forcing a piece in to make it fit! The reason why we force a piece in, is because we are missing the lid to the box! The box "lid" contains the finished image of the puzzle.

As only 3 percent of people have a definite goal (or the lid to the box of the success puzzle). They are the only ones who manage to achieve their definition of success in good time. Everyone has their own personal definition of success, and if you were to stop and ask a hundred people on the street, you would no doubt get a hundred different answers, most of which do not work for them. If it was working for the majority, you would naturally see more happy, wealthy, enthusiastic people. Next time you drive past a bus stop just check out the faces of the people waiting in line. Any walk or drive to work on a Monday morning will also validate my point!

Success in life is governed by universal laws that have been discovered thousands of years ago. The interesting thing about these laws though are that you have to prove them to yourself before you see the real value in them and accept them.

Earl Nightingale's definition of success is probably the best version I have ever heard and it goes like this,

"Success is the progressive realisation of a worthy ideal."

Earl Nightingale arrived at this definition in 1959 after seventeen years of intensive research. If a person is moving toward a predetermined goal and knows where to go, then that person is successful. If a person does not know which direction they want to go in life, then that person is a failure.

"Success is the progressive realisation of a worthy ideal."

Therefore, who succeeds?

The only person who succeeds is the person who is progressively realizing a *worthy* ideal. The person who says, "I'm going to become this, or do this"... and then begins to work towards it.

What I've found over the years is that most people get the formula mixed up, mentally asking "Am I worthy of the goal or dream I'm going after?" Of course that's the wrong question. The real question should be "Is the goal I'm going after worthy of me?" Big difference. Is the goal really worth spending possibly my entire life devoted to realising it? The truth is that whatever you decide to do, life is pretty short and you and I are trading every day of our lives for something.

Have you ever wondered why so many men and women work so hard and have no fun, without ever achieving anything in particular? Why others do not seem to work hard at all and yet get everything? We sometimes think it is the magic touch or pure luck. We often say, "Everything they touch turns to gold." Have you ever noticed that a person who becomes successful tends to continue this pattern of success? Or on the other hand, how a person who fails seems to continually fail?

Success is not the result of making money; making money is the result of success and the money you earn is in direct proportion to the quality and quantity of service delivered. If we are not giving much, we don't deserve to get much. Pretty simple!

George Bernard Shaw once said:

"People are always blaming their circumstances for what they are. I don't believe in circumstances. The people who get on in this world are the people who get up and look for the circumstances they want, and if they can't find them, make them."

Now, it stands to reason that a person who is thinking about a concrete and worthwhile goal is going to reach it, because that's what he's thinking about. And we become what we think about.

Conversely, the man who has no goal, who doesn't know where he's going, allows and attracts thoughts which cause confusion, anxiety and doubt. His life becomes one of frustration, fear and worry.

And if he thinks about nothing.....by default he becomes nothing. This is really fundamental stuff, but missed by most people.

So decide now. What is it you want? Plant your goal in your mind. It's the most important decision you'll ever make in your entire life. All you've got to do is plant that seed in your mind, care for it daily and work steadily toward your goal, and it will become a reality.

So how do you begin? Well, seeing how we are talking about money in this chapter, let's use that as an example. Most people who are reading this book would probably like more money. The problem is not that they can't have it, it's that they aren't aware of the necessity to think differently about it. Most people who would like to change their financial situation condemn and restrict themselves by thinking one of two ways:

1. They presume they have to work harder and longer doing pretty much the exact same thing as they are now.

2. They don't *really* believe they can have more, and therefore never *really* think about how they could.

Most people feel as though they have to know all the steps of the "How" first, *before* they do anything. They hypnotise themselves into thinking that they already know what will and won't work for them based on of all of their prior experience. In my experience most people (at best) try one way, one time and that's all the evidence they need to make a judgement as to whether something will work for them or not.

To illustrate the point, in figure 11 on page 136, a person earning £30,000 a year is thinking £30,000 a year thoughts. Therefore the *only* thoughts that person can attract are similar and like thoughts. The only things they can accept, related to money are £30,000 a year ideas, people and opportunities. They get mired in their own paradigm of potential because they don't understand how their mind really works. They want to earn or make more, but they continue to think thoughts at the exact same level at which they are currently stuck. The mind is a magnet and corresponds to our dominant mental ruling state. If you want to earn say, £330,000 a year, you have to start to raise your level of awareness (or consciousness) immediately to that new higher level of £330,000. You have to hold the image on the screen of your mind of the £330,000 lifestyle, even though all of your existing reality is demonstrating and reinforcing a £30,000 lifestyle. Only then will your mind start to attract all the necessary bits of information, resources and plans to make the higher income or lifestyle a new reality.

Higher Level of Consciousness

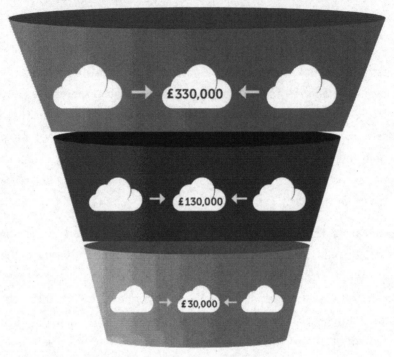

Lower Level of Consciousness

Figure 11

Penthouse Please

You could think of the diagram above as floor levels in a top west end hotel in London.

Let's pretend that previous to arriving at the hotel you had to fill in a basic on-line questionnaire. In this questionnaire was your annual income, how much you've improved year on year, how happy you are and how full of expectation and real belief you have in your future for the coming years. On arrival the receptionist looks through your answers, has a quick look up from the computer, and then hands you the keys to your room. Your answers to the questions dictate your level of awareness and therefore what level or floor you get to stay on. You get room 520. That means the receptionist (who happens to be your subconscious) has given you the physical room number 520 based on your own evaluation of yourself and your awareness of your mind to, *"Think Smart-Live Rich!"*

After years of going to the same hotel and being frustrated at always getting stuck with a room with the same view year after year, you demand to have a room higher up. Other people get to stay in rooms higher up you protest, why not me? The receptionist apologises and lets you know that she is really sorry, but your own evaluation and awareness must dictate the floor level you get to stay on.

Until this changes there is nothing more she can do about it.

After so many years of being frustrated of seeing the same fifth floor view year after year, it suddenly dawns on you what you need to do to move up the levels. You have to go there in your mind-*first.*

You start to imagine what it must be like to stay in a top floor apartment - the penthouse suite. With its classic London themed art décor, marble foyer, guest bathroom and wet bar. 60-inch HDTV, in-room entertainment system with surround sound. His and hers Italian marble bath with whirlpool, glass enclosed steam shower, automatic drapery and remote controls.

With these images of pure luxury and a view of the city to die for, you start to get emotionally attached to this picture and the lifestyle that would naturally accompany it. You don't want it as a one off, somewhere where you come once every five years and then panic about the expense on your credit-card, you want it all the time. The more you hold the emotional image of what you want in your mind, the more you trigger off thought vibrations of energy that are harmonious to you completing this picture. Your subconscious mind has a new "target" to aim for and deliberately works on your behalf (often behind the scenes) to fulfil this image, in exactly the same way as it did before to keep you stuck on the fifth floor. Ways and means *only now* become apparent as to how you can live like this and you start to move up the levels.

The point I'm making is simple;

Until you increase your level of awareness you can't permanently experience anything other than your current results are demonstrating to you.

Einstein said, "We cannot solve our problems with the same thinking we used when we created them." Because most people don't comprehend this very simple idea at the emotional level of understanding, they continue to get frustrated with where they are. So what do we have to do?

First: It is understanding emotionally as well as intellectually that we literally become what we think about; that we must control our thoughts if we're to control our lives. It's understanding fully that... "as ye sow, so shall ye reap."

Second: It's cutting away all fetters from the mind and permitting it to soar as it was divinely designed to do. It's the realisation that your limitations are self-imposed and that the opportunities for you today are enormous beyond belief. It's rising above your own narrow-minded pettiness and paradigms.

Third: It's using all your understanding to force yourself to think "higher" on your own problems, to set a definite and clearly defined goal for yourself. To let your marvellous mind think about your goal from all possible angles; to let your imagination speculate freely upon many different possible solutions. To refuse to believe that there are any circumstances sufficiently strong enough to defeat you in the accomplishment of your purpose. To act promptly and decisively when your course is clear. And to keep constantly aware of the fact that you are, at this moment, standing in the middle of your own "acres of diamonds." Everything you want is already here, your just not aware of it......yet.

EXERCISES

What is your personal definition of Success?

_____

_____

_____

_____

What belief stops you from living this way?

_____

_____

_____

_____

Who could help you?

_____

_____

_____

_____

Chapter 6

The Cybernetic Mind

We live in a society which has arbitrarily decided that the measure of our success is often judged solely by the size of our bank account or by our ability to earn money. The media perpetuates this belief daily through TV, internet and film. This is not the real and true measure of success as you know, but it is the measure used most in free societies. Down through the ages money has been the reward for achievement.

"Show me the Money!" Inevitably, this attitude has produced a success/failure concept which is obviously based on a false premise. Up until you die and your brain ceases to function you can totally change any aspect of your life. Up until the grim reaper pays you a visit, there are *only degrees of success.*

"We act, behave and feel according to what we consider our SELF-IMAGE to be and we do not deviate from this pattern."
– Dr Maxwell Maltz

If you were to look at the bottom of the "success scale," the drunken tramp on Skid Row would be considered to be one of the biggest failures of our society. And yet think about it for a moment. At what he wants to do, which is to get booze, he is eminently successful. The ingenuity with which he pursues and accomplishes his goal is remarkable. The fascinating thing from a psychological point of view is that in my opinion there are no such things as drug, alcohol or substance problems in the United Kingdom at all. I believe what we really have is a *self-esteem* and *self-image* problem. The real question that we should be asking is what drives people to start these activities in the *first* place? The program that runs deep in the tramp -

"get booze by any means," never lets him down. It's also the same process used by the Hollywood actress hooked on coke. Whether his goal is a good one, or worth pursuing, is not a matter of success, but of values. The point I'm making is this: *you can use the exact same mechanism to accomplish whatever goal you set for yourself.*

Even when values are shared the "either-or" distinction between success and failure is never valid. The idea that the person earning £25,000 a year is less successful than the person earning £25,000 a month, is only valid *if* you want to earn £25,000 a month and value money highly! It's more about *degrees* of success than whether you are a winner or not. Top performers are *always* looking to improve and frequently ask themselves how can I stay permanently motivated to do the things I know I must do? What is motivation exactly? I define it as follows:

> **Motivation is the deliberate control of purposeful behaviour towards specific goals.**

Contained within this definition are two concepts of crucial importance; *goals and control.*

The real promise of Mind Cybernetics is goal achievement faster, easier and less stressful than ever before.

Cybernetics Explained

Cybernetics was originated by Norbert Weiner, an American professor of mathematics at MIT. It was World War II that caused Weiner to turn his attention to the development of computers and to the investigation of how the control of anti-aircraft guns could be improved upon. Weiner realised that a very important factor involved in improving the performance of gunner and gun against pilot and plane was what engineers call "Feedback." This led Weiner to a complete investigation of Feedback techniques and under what circumstances Feedback mechanisms could break down.

The computer, guided missile systems and the automatic pilot in a Boeing 747 are the results of physicists and mathematicians studying the science of Cybernetics. We have studied the human brain, copied its function and put it in a machine. This *mechanical* brain responds automatically to signals or input, performing complex calculations in a split second. In turn, the computer sciences have helped us to better understand and appreciate our personal "in built" *mental* computer as well.

Cybernetics comes from the Greek word *Kybernetes* meaning *helmsman*. It is the *steering* of goals or information to a successful conclusion or desired end result. The brain and nervous system are under the automatic control of the mind. The brain is *not* the mind. The mind *uses* the brain as its servant just like the owner of the penthouse suite uses a concierge service in a top Mayfair hotel. Just as a computer or missile can be programmed, your brain can be programmed automatically to increase skills and performance.

Simply stated, Mind Cybernetics is the study of your internal guidance system working with the brain and nervous system that responds to signals or information. The success or failure of the system depends entirely upon the information it receives. Faulty programming causes the system to miss its target and fail. Accurate programming allows the system to function correctly and thus succeed in its mission or goal.

The Principles of Mind Cybernetics

Every person who aspires to be a top performer must grasp the importance of developing strong mental attitudes. And yet many people will have in the past been on some type of chest beating "positive thinking" type course in order to improve in this area. Chances are they will have learnt some helpful information, and then not acted on it. Why? Because *positive thinking cannot be used effectively* as a patch or Band-Aid on the same old ineffective concept of "self."

In fact, it is literally impossible to really think positively about a situation, as long as you hold a negative concept of self-relative to that particular area. Numerous sessions and experiments have shown that once the concept of self is changed, other things consistent with this new self-concept are accomplished easily and without strain.

Your subconscious mind has a goal-striving *servo-mechanism* built into it which works in conjunction with the brain and nervous system.

Your servo-mechanism is an automatic device that uses error-sensing negative feedback to correct your performance of a given skill or objective. This servo mechanism, controlled by the self-image, works tirelessly to guide you towards whatever goals or objectives it is clearly given, much like guided missile technology. This servo mechanism has a split personality however, it can work either as an automatic success mechanism or an automatic failure mechanism, depending on what "work order" it is given, and what is communicated to it through the self-image. This mechanism has no built in bias in one direction or another, it just accepts whatever you tell it to do.

In short, if the goals that you attempt to convey to this mechanism are inconsistent with the self-image, they are **rejected** or **modified**. By discovering how to alter and modify your self-concept *first*, you end its conflict with your goals. If you *then* add new "Success Information" to your mind and it's in harmony with this new self-concept, the new goal, image or behaviour is finally accepted by the subconscious and the changes and results take place naturally and effortlessly.

Top network marketing trainers and leaders tell me that they soon stop telling prospective distributors that they can earn £10,000 a month in network marketing. The problem is that few new prospects actually *believe* that the figures quoted are doable for them *personally*. Yes, they could see how someone *else* could have the lavish lifestyle, the Porsche 911 and the £60,000 a month income but not them. It is far better to make claims of say £500-£1000 a month, as it's more in line with the belief system of the average Joe. It's not that large numbers aren't doable, it's just that the self-concept is rejecting the idea. It's just too far away from the current reality. Once the trainers reduced the income claims, conversion rates into the business increased dramatically. By discovering how to alter your self-image you align it with your goals, rather than have it work *against* your goals.

So, your brain and nervous system constitute a goal-striving mechanism that operates automatically to achieve a certain goal, very much like a submarine torpedo or heat seeking missile seeks and steers its way to its target. Your subconscious mind functions both as a guidance system to *automatically* steer you in the right direction to achieve certain goals or to make corrective responses and changes based on certain "negative" feedback.

In Mind Cybernetics we are learning to more effectively communicate with and through the self-image, so as to better control the "success mechanism."

For example, when a target is known such as an enemy ship, the objective of the self-guided torpedo is to reach it and destroy it. Such machines must "know" the target they are shooting for. It must have some sort of propulsion system that propels it forward in the general direction of its target as well. It must be equipped with "senses" (radar, sonar etc) that relays information back from the target. These senses keep the torpedo informed when it is on the correct course (positive feedback) and when it commits an error and gets off course (negative feedback). If the torpedo goes too far off to the right, the corrective mechanism automatically causes the rudder to "steer" the torpedo back to the left. The torpedo achieves its goal by *going forward, making errors and continually correcting them* by a series of zigzags.

Boom! Target located.

At the moment I'm just watching my eight-month-old baby girl, Eliza use the same process to "locate" her rattle. Because she is so young, she has very little stored information in the brain to draw upon, so her hand zigzags back and forth, over and around the rattle until she finds or "gropes" her way to it. As learning and repetition takes place, the correction becomes more and more refined. We see the same process when babies try to walk or when a teenager is learning to drive. When you first learnt to drive you were probably all over the place and used excessive force on the brakes when getting into potential danger. The more practice and experience you have (to a degree!) the better your driving gets. As the old adage goes, someone who has forty years-experience may have the same *one* years - experience *repeated* forty times!

Once a correct or successful response has been accomplished, it is remembered for future use. The servo-mechanism duplicates this successful response with future objectives. It has *learned* the process. It remembers its successes and "forgets" its failures and repeats its successful action as a habit. This is why top performers are so adept at the skills important to their success. Top sales professionals make things look so easy because their responses have become so ingrained like grooves in a record, held in the subconscious.

We marvel when watching a Hollywood blockbuster where there is a deadly alien invasion. The US Air Force sends in a formation of F-15 Eagle's, in an attempt to blow up the mother-ship full of evil mutants. The guided missiles attack and destroy the mother-ship with incredible accuracy and the hero of course gets off with the leading lady. (Unless there is an invisible shield of course, then you're screwed. These pesky aliens learn well you know!).

Think about a normal weekend game of Premiership football. It's the same cybernetic process in action. The right winger nutmegs the oppositions left back, has a sneaky look up to locate his team mate in the box and curls the ball high and hard into the penalty area. To "compute" where the ball is going to be in advance, or the point of interception, the striker has to take into account the speed and weight of the ball, its direction, wind swirl, humidity, how hard the winger kicked it in the first place, (initial velocity), and the rate of progressive *decrease* in velocity all at the same time!

The striker must time his run to perfection in order to intercept the cross and stick it in the back of the net. The brain uses all of its "sensors" to measure the deviation from the ball being kicked, to the point of impact by way of feedback into the nervous system. It takes all this complicated data, and compares it with previously stored data (memories of other crosses in the past, *especially* from the same winger) all the way back from primary school to the present moment.

A decision is made in an instant and the brain says, "Get ready to run..... now!"

Your Money Thermostat

We all have a 'Money Thermostat' inside our subconscious mind that is set for how much money we believe is right for us or that we are capable of earning. This thermostat is usually set rather early in our childhood through our belief system, made up from our different experiences with money. Once this is set, your cybernetic mechanism continues to make sure you don't stray "off track" your habitual level of income too much either way.

Also created at an early age are the tapes that play over and over in our subconscious minds. As you know, we probably heard our parents saying things like "Money doesn't grow on trees" "You've got to work hard in life to make it" "We can't afford it" as well as positive statements such as, "You can be anything you want to be" "You're the greatest" and "You're so smart." These comments help to create our beliefs about what is possible and also set our income thermostats at their particular level. However most people have an imbalance towards the negative.

We also might see things at an early age such as our dad coming home tired and dirty after working a tough physical job all day. This often creates a tape running in our subconscious that says it's not right to make money sitting at a computer inside where it's warm, dry and clean and not sweating from physical labour. That tape says that something's wrong with making money this way and that we have to sweat, be physically tired and get dirty to make a living.

Many people who start businesses do a lot of networking and pound the streets in order to get the business up and running, but soon find that when they are making roughly the same as they were when they were employed, they back off and coast. This is because although they have the capacity through leverage to massively increase their income, they don't, because they haven't altered this "inner image" thermostat. This doesn't just happen in business, it happens in many areas of life.

According to sporting charity X-Pro, Many footballers face serious financial problems when they get injured or retire. The group claims as many as three in five Premier League footballers face bankruptcy within five years of retiring from the game. Of course, most reports will cite that they got into bad investments or weren't really financially savvy, but the reality is that the problems started in the mind-first. They never mentally re-calibrated to the vastly higher levels of income they received whilst playing, and because of this, they made bad investments or in some cases ended up blowing it all.

Our actions each day actually play out exactly what is needed to do to be congruent with the level our thermostat is set at. This is why in business the ONLY way to truly make more money in life and to hang onto it is to raise our income thermostats. Jim Rohn, the American entrepreneur, author and motivational speaker said it best when he wrote, "If you won a million dollars, the first thing to do is to become a millionaire." Of course what he meant was, if you are not comfortable at a subconscious level with that much money, you will absolutely begin to sabotage yourself until your outside net worth is once again in line with your *inside* net worth. This is why most lottery winners eventually end up back at the same financial level they were before the win.

Our subconscious keeps our actions in line with our thermostat by controlling our conscious action. In sales the process is exactly the same. The subconscious ALWAYS wins the war. It's virtually impossible to expect to just consciously "try harder" and somehow expect to turn our sales around. Consistent profitable selling has to happen through the subconscious mind. We have to let go of the process at a conscious level and imbed the new programs at a subconscious level.

EXERCISES

What is Cybernetics?

_____

_____

_____

_____

What amount is your Money Thermostat Stuck at?

_____

_____

_____

How long has it been stuck there for?

_____

_____

_____

How much should you be earning?

_____

_____

_____

_____

Chapter 7

Neurogenics™

By now you should be convinced that the most critical factor in determining how you will perform in any area of your life is by altering your self-concept of how you see yourself at the subconscious level. To alter any behaviour on the outside without first changing core beliefs on the inside would be temporary at best and always in conflict with "who you really are." This is the main reason fast and effortless change has up until now, been a problem. Enormous resistance to change occurs when you try to do something that is not in harmony with this "inner image." Nearly all other programs for behavioural change attempt to use reprogramming techniques without eliminating core beliefs first (see the Handbrake Effect in Chapter 4).

Imagine your subconscious mind as a large nightclub in the middle of Newcastle. As with most nightclubs there is only one door at the front. The front entrance is protected by the doorman who represents your conscious mind. His primary role is to limit entry according to "desirability."

When you were born, the whole club was empty because it was so early and the doorman let in anyone with a pulse. As you grew older and experienced new interpretations and events, your "club" began to fill up with a variety of beliefs about yourself and your world. These beliefs joined together to form your exclusive club, determining your personality and behaviour. Eventually this executive club became so selective that it began to tell the doorman just who could come in and join the group, and who gets to go home with a taxi and a pizza. In other words when your subconscious mind didn't feel comfortable with a potential applicant (a new belief), it was refused access. The club was exercising its right to only allow in new members of similar stature to long term members (old beliefs).

The contents of your club represent the total programming your subconscious mind has been subjected to up until now and has casting vote on all new members. The word on the street is, if you're not like us, you're not coming in.

Here's the question. If you were a potential club member (and a really positive belief) but you kept on getting turfed away at the club door every night, how long would it take before you decided it just wasn't worth the effort of trying? Two, three, maybe ten times? Most people haven't got the persistence to constantly fight the old conditioning in their subconscious, so they give up, and give up pretty quickly. After all, who needs the frustration?

Red Velvet Rope Policy

What if you'd been out of Newcastle for a while (Maybe you've been trying Sunderland instead!) and you come back one night to try your luck again. As you approach the doorman, you expect to be rejected so you pull back your shoulders, puff out your chest and give it your best patter. However this time, to your surprise, he gently smiles, pulls back the red velvet rope and gestures you inside. You enter without any fuss or drama and take your rightful place at the VIP table where you should have been years ago. What's changed? How come this time you get let in so easily? Turns out there has been a change of management. The new management has recently got rid of any old members (old beliefs) that didn't fit their new objectives of wealth and success. Now the new members they want to attract slip in with ease because there is no resistance. These are the type of people they want. They emptied the club of all the rubbish first, *before* giving the place a makeover and attracting better and higher quality clients. As the club thrived the word spread and soon the place was rammed with wealthy and successful people (similar beliefs).

As you can see with my example, its much, much easier to get the new beliefs you want, if you empty your mind of all the rubbish that is in there first. If rubbish has been allowed entrance then rubbish is stored in the memory. The most prominent feature of old rubbish is the smell. If rubbish has been stored in your mind, then the unfortunate doorman at the front door acquires the same characteristic-he begins to smell as well. He can't help but smell because he guards the only door the stench can exit from-your conscious mind.

This gives you some understanding of the serious problem many people face: a smouldering pile of crap in their mind that is protected by an obedient, well trained guard who has very clear instructions to only allow in more of the same.

When accelerating successful behaviours we have to find some way to bypass the guard, (your conscious mind) as it currently exists with all of its biases and perceptions. Remember it is standing proud and protective of all the negative and destructive beliefs it has *already* entered into your subconscious mind. It will not give in easily just because you demand it. Force usually doesn't work with any doorman! It will reject and intercept anything it views as new or different, as contrary to whatever is already acceptable and compatible with your prior programming.

If you recall, it was Dr Maxwell Maltz's view that self-concept psychology was the most successful technique for dramatic improvement and change in personality. He discovered that the subconscious always works like a goal orientated mechanism to bring into physical reality the goals that you have planted in memory. The subconscious doesn't joke, and is totally impersonal. It processes limiting beliefs and churns them into realities exactly the same as all your positive beliefs.

As you've discovered, **Success information + Motivation** by itself is not the answer. Logic and reason alone will not bring about the accelerated changes you need in order to move ahead fast. It is not enough to keep telling yourself, "I am confident and successful" or "I can achieve anything I want," when deep down, *your subconscious does not believe you*. It's kind of like sticking a plaster on a broken leg-it's useless. If you experience a multitude of self-doubts, beliefs and fears, your early programming is your primary obstacle to success.

All of your potential exists at a higher level of consciousness.

Research has shown that it takes between 26-30 days to begin to form a new habit. In fact, one of these research studies is an incredible illustration of the physiological connection between time and "habits."

Back in the early days of the space program, NASA designed an experiment to determine the physiological and psychological effects of the spatial disorientation the astronauts would experience in the weightless environment of space.

NASA scientists outfitted each of the astronauts with a pair of convex goggles which flipped everything in their field of vision 180 degrees. In other words, their world was literally turned upside down. The astronauts had to wear the goggles 24 hours a day, 7 days per week—even when they were asleep.

Although they experienced physical symptoms of anxiety and stress initially – elevated blood pressure, respiration and other vital signs – they gradually adapted to their new "realities." On the 26th day of the experiment however, something amazing happened for one of the astronauts. His world turned right-side up again even though he continued to wear the goggles 24 hours a day!

Between days 26-30, the same thing happened for each of the remaining astronauts.

After 30 days, each of their brains had formed enough new neural connections to turn this "lie" into the truth. They had literally re-created reality. They extended the experiment to learn more about this and interestingly, when they completed the experiment and the astronauts took off the goggles, everything turned wrong side up again!

They also found that if the goggles were taken off during that three to four week period that this event would not occur. It takes the brain this long to build the new neurons. If we stop the process during the 30 days then we need to start all over again.

As we learn new things new synaptic connections are formed in our brains, by repetition, association and emotion. The more connections there are, the more likely it is that this memory will stay strong for us habitually.

In order to change a habit, it is crucial that you put systems in place to insure you follow the new behaviour you have chosen. Otherwise, without thinking you will revert to the old behaviour!

After 30 days of conscious, intentional, deliberate thought and effort it gets easier and easier, and by 30-40 days it is very much a part of who you are – a new habit; only this time it's one that is serving you and moving you toward your goals. From this point forward you're likely to be in the habit of deliberate conscious creation and will continue to program yourself with everything necessary to reach your goals.

It's important to understand that it's not good enough to just decide to break a bad habit. Once the bad habit is gone, what is it going to be replaced with?

Nature abhors a vacuum and releasing a bad habit leaves a void that will be filled with something. So, if you do not consciously and deliberately replace a habit that it not serving you with one that will, then I can guarantee you that the void will be filled by another "bad" habit.

Old Paradigm

Beliefs take ages to change and its hard work. The longer the belief has been stuck in your subconscious, the longer it's going to take to integrate an opposite belief. This outdated view goes back to endless visits to the psychiatrists, laying on a comfortable sofa constantly reliving aspects of your childhood. Scientists would believe the brain was hardwired and fixed like a mechanical machine.

New Paradigm

Thanks to the fairly recent discovery of neuroplasticity, we now know that the brain is continually making new neural pathways in the brain according to its environment. It doesn't matter whether that "environment" is observed outside the physical body or is "made real" by the faculty of imagination on the screen of the mind on the "inside." The subconscious aspect of your mind where lasting change takes place can't tell the difference. Eliminating the beliefs you don't want is similar to revising a document in a computer. It doesn't take any longer to change a document that has been in your computer for ten years than it does for one that's been in ten minutes. Just like a computer, if you change the information that it holds, you change the performance and capabilities.

So what's the answer to integrating new beliefs?

There is a tried and tested method that works. I call it **Neurogenic Conditioning™**. "Neuro," being related to the study of the brain and nervous system and "Genics," having been adapted from the work of Dr. Johannes H.Schultz, a German neurologist who developed the work of Autogenics. Autogenic simply means, "produced from within" or self-generating. In total it amounts to an advanced method of mind control now used by many Olympic and professional athletes as part of their rigorous training program.

It's a three dimensional technique that combines progressive relaxation, positive affirmation, and creative visualisation. It also allows you to tap deep into your subconscious mind and bypass the conscious doorman.

Neurogenic Conditioning™ is an accelerated learning technique that involves a combination of repeating a positive statement to yourself while in a state of deep relaxation (the alpha brainwave state) and combining it with an associated visualisation and emotion that is representative of exactly what you want to accomplish-either a particular goal or outcome. This leads us to an explanation of the **Neurogenic Conditioning™** process and the alpha brain wave state. It also explains in more depth how and why you got programmed so easily when you were a kid.

The **SHIFT B.E.L.I.E.F.S System™** and the **Neurogenic Conditioning™** process combined, gives you what I believe to be one of the fastest, if not *the* fastest behavioural change and accelerated results systems in the world today.

*Simply put, the **SHIFT B.E.L.I.E.F.S System™** eliminates the unwanted beliefs held in the mind, whilst **Neurogenic Conditioning™** grows and develops new empowering beliefs, effectively re-wiring the neural pathways in your brain to support you in the achievement of your future goals.*

Getting into Flow

Generally we have five levels of brain-wave activity: gamma, alpha, beta, theta and delta. However, to keep things simple we are only going to look at the four main brainwave states to get a better understanding of the early programming that took place.

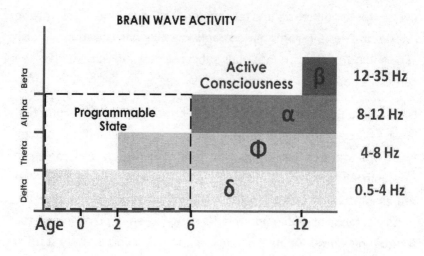

Figure 12

Beta

The brain is constantly generating a series of pulses of electrical energy that reflect its level of activity. Most of the time these pulses are fairly rapid, between 12-35+Hz or cycles per second. These higher frequencies are called beta waves, and they are the ones that you are generating to read this book. Beta waves are associated with being fully awake and mentally alert, and involve such activities as talking, listening and concentrating.

Alpha

Slower brain wave frequencies, those between 8-12 Hz are called alpha waves. They are more prominent when on the edge of sleep, a sort of dream like state. Alpha states can often be induced when driving your car on a road you know really well. You, probably like me have often driven your car for many miles and wondered how on earth you actually made it to your destination! You can't consciously remember much of the journey, but somehow you managed to get where you wanted to. This is when alpha was driving on your behalf. When the car in front of you suddenly brakes, you quickly flip back into the wide awake state of beta, and come out of your slightly dazed state. When the brain is in the alpha state (such as driving home from work) the body is usually relaxed and the two brain hemispheres of the brain are "happier together" and more coherent. This creates increased whole brain functioning that is often associated with high performance and creativity. This is when great ideas are more likely to slip in.

Theta

From about the ages of 2 years old to 6 years old our brain is in a predominantly theta brain wave state, (4-8Hz) which represents dreaming and contemplation. This is when we easily create imaginative worlds, turning pots and pans into rocket launchers and sticks into wizards wands!

Delta

For the first two years of our lives we are predominantly in a delta brainwave pattern (0.5-4Hz). Although this is deep sleep for adults, infants and very young children produce delta waves when they are conscious. At this age we are downloading massive amounts of emotional and environmental information through our five senses, recording everything in the subconscious mind for future use. This was natures deliberate design in order to us to learn what we needed to very quickly.

As you can see in the brain-wave diagram (figure 12), during the first six years of our lives we are in a very programmable brain-wave state. This is why young children can speak multiple languages at the same time if they are exposed to them on a daily basis. Information and learned behaviours are adopted simply by exposure and observation. This early programming also includes downloading core information relative to our self-concept and to the type of person we believe we are and the capabilities we have. The truth is that the majority of us are continually running programs in the mind now that have been downloaded from our early environment. This would be great if the environment at that time was positive, wealthy and encouraging and more importantly if we "interpreted" these events as positive beliefs about us and the world. But we don't always do that.

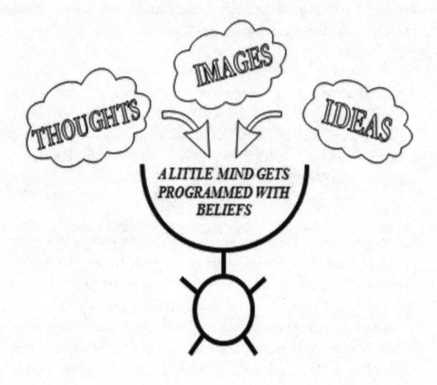

Figure 13

As you can see in figure 13, when we are young the subconscious mind is wide open to suggestion. The conscious faculties haven't yet been fully developed, so information just flows freely in to the subconscious. It's not until around the age of six that your conscious mind can start to reason with some of the information being presented to it and can start to reject some of it if it's not helpful.

The real challenge with this human system is that the limited beliefs we have interpreted at a very young age are *already* in the subconscious before the age of six and will continue to express themselves as "truths" until we actually eliminate them and replace them with more empowering beliefs. At around six years old the conscious mind starts to filter all new information its exposed to and rejects information that is "unlike" that which it was previously programmed with. This is why most people reject information that could really help them. They have in effect turned deaf, dumb and blind to any ideas that are not in harmony with their pre-conceived ideas. Any area that you are struggling with continually is due to a mind programmed with limiting beliefs relative to that area.

As an adult, whilst you are in the alpha state, you have improved access to your subconscious mind, the power core representing unlimited potential. In this brain-wave state the way is no longer blocked by the conscious mind which edits out any thoughts deemed inconsistent with your current beliefs.

The alpha state is experienced naturally just before falling off to sleep and just waking up. These are ideal times to start to re-program your subconscious with the beliefs of your choosing.

Another powerful option is to *induce* an alpha state deliberately by conscious effort at a suitable time during the day by practicing progressive relaxation and implementing **Neurogenic Conditioning™.**

Neurogenic Conditioning™ is a simple seven step process.

1. Find a quiet place where you won't be disturbed for 20 minutes.

2. Cross your legs at the ankles and put your left hand on top of your right hand whilst holding them both over your sternum. Close your eyes and turn them slightly upwards towards your forehead. Research shows these two actions accelerate the alpha brain-wave state.

3. Relax your mind and body by using the 4:7:8 breathing technique. Breath in for four seconds through your nose, hold it for seven seconds and exhale through the mouth for eight seconds. Do this

process three times. Now count backwards from 50 to 1. In time you can reduce the countdown to as little as 5-1.

4. Hold on the screen of your mind your success goal already achieved, with as much detail as possible. See the individual behavioural changes you want and the specific belief you'd like to integrate into your subconscious. If your mind gets distracted, keep pulling it back to the image you want and hold it still.

5. Accept this scene fully and the change it represents as already being realised.

6. Immerse yourself in the positive feelings this picture or image generates.

7. Mentally repeat a suitable and applicable positive affirmation over and over again in conjunction with your image. Hold this image/affirmation/emotion for 15-20 minutes.

The Neurogenic process involves three essential elements at the same time.

Visualisation,

Affirmation,

and Emotion.

You must incorporate all of these elements at the same time in order for the process to be most effective. The reason why it works is because you are replicating a situation that the subconscious thinks is real. As I've said before your subconscious can't tell the difference between a real (external) event or imagined (internal) event. When you think about your future success you literally *experience* it now internally; in other words, you create an image in your mind that is entered into the memory banks of your subconscious and this creates a new neural path in the brain. The more you do **Neurogenic Conditioning™** the more the neural pathway gets integrated. The path gets wider, longer and stronger, just the same as a well-trodden path through a forest or country walk. Using the process you can replicate the exact experience you want on the *outside* by first experiencing it on the *inside*. This is what it means to be the master of your fate and the captain of your soul. Because most people are exposed to different external stimuli, and have varying degrees of ability to make the interpretations of their choosing, this process gives them the internal control needed to "guide" the subconscious to their desired "success" target.

Your current individual behavioural "targets" are responsible for the automatic behaviour of your subconscious. If you don't like what your results are in any area of your life you need to create new targets for your subconscious to "locate."

For example, if you don't like the fact that you eat when you're bored and do it automatically it's because you have this "outcome" as a stored target in your subconscious mind. If you don't like the income you get, it's because you have this level of income as a stored target in your subconscious. After all, the joke is they often call it "take-home" pay because you'd be embarrassed to take it anywhere else!

Neurogenic Conditioning™ allows you to design and create improved behavioural targets into your subconscious reality, making these the new automatically chosen pathways for your cybernetic guidance system to follow. The feelings or emotions that you generate from your imagined success images drive the new belief deep into your subconscious reality. Your relaxed alpha state simply allows you to do this without conflict from your critical conscious mind.

Get excited, because for once YOU are going to be master and commander, YOU are the deliberate programmer, YOU are the dominant force in your life. If you are like the millions of people on the planet who weren't programmed for success then you must take on this responsibility for yourself.

As you continually repeat this process you'll find over time you can get into the alpha state faster and faster. Remember though, right now this is you at your worst! Relax with the process, don't try and force it to work, allow it to work.

In the same way that your incredible mind has been programmed by self-limiting beliefs, these success sabotaging beliefs can be permanently eliminated. **Neurogenic Conditioning™** then paves the way open to the integration of your new empowering beliefs to grow in a weed free environment. This gives us one of the fastest behavioural and accelerated results system in the world today.

This process helps you discover latent talents, skills and resources buried deep within you, brings them to the surface and puts them on display. A typical conditioning session aims towards the integration of a new **belief** and new **behaviour** which changes your **expectations of yourself**. These new expectations cause you to act *externally* in a manner consistent with your new *internal* success images.

80/20 Visualisation

During the visualisation part of the process focus on being fully associated with the experience 80 percent of the time. So if you were doing a presentation for example and you were stood on a stage at the front of a room, you would be looking at the audience's faces rather than looking at yourself at the front of the room. This reflects you as the initiator of the activity rather than a spectator.

For the remaining 20 percent of your visualisation see yourself as if you were a spectator looking at yourself on stage. The reason why you want to do it both ways is so you can give yourself complete 360 degree feedback to your subconscious-giving you the best possible outcome.

You must remember one critical point in this regard. You are able to bring into reality an act or event only to the degree that you are able to picture it clearly and in every detail in your imagination *first*.

In other words, if you cannot believe it and see it in your mind, you will not be able to actualise it in your experience. You will continue to bumble around, hazy-fantazy, not knowing exactly what you are trying to achieve. Research shows that you forget around 90 percent of everything you hear once in about twenty-four hours. But if you see and hear the same thing repeated over and over again, you tend to remember it. This type of learning experience takes advantage of what is called "spaced repetition" and it is the type represented by the Neurogenic process.

Many experienced public speakers are known to run through their presentation successfully in their imagination before ever giving it to a live audience. Looking out through their eyes, they see the audience responding and being receptive to their advice or remarks in the exact way they want. When they are performing live, they are simply going through their routine one more time. Their cybernetic system goes to work to have them fulfil this "success target,"(a great presentation) in the precise way they have previously envisioned it. To the degree that they were able to believe and see themselves doing well and affect the audience in the way they wanted, they will determine their physical results. Their nervous system simple "retraces" the neural imprints etched onto their mental map. The quality of their performance-their behavioural response-is totally predictable. Their live experience is just as successful as the map or blueprint they have previously conditioned themselves with, in their imagination.

Using **Neurogenic Conditioning™** in this way means that you can see that your future is virtually unlimited. Whatever image you can create and hold in your mind on a continual basis, you can be, do or have. You need only decide who it is you really want to be and what it is you want to do. You become your ideal self-concept by imagining being ideal in your mind first. Learn to lean in the direction you want to go. The reality is this: Anything that you continually hold on the screen of the mind affects and directs your cybernetic mechanism. It understands these images as targets to aim for, and uses them as a command to get you there. The main reason why people don't get the results they want isn't that hard to work out. They don't decide fully what the goal, target or outcome should be, and continually confuse the cybernetic mechanism by allowing outside circumstances to dictate what images they hold on the screen of their mind. In simple terms, they allow the outside circumstances, events and results to control their internal images-creating a never ending loop of mediocrity.

You must start to realise the many talents and abilities you possess that are now being denied existence by self-limiting beliefs. By permanently eliminating these beliefs and replacing them with beliefs and images that support your goals, you can accelerate ahead at an incredibly fast pace. This is simply because there is no external resistance to your internal practice. Using the techniques described in this book you can consciously and deliberately change your most intimate beliefs about yourself and set your sights on any success "target" you choose.

EXERCISES

What brainwave state is best for using Neurogenics?

_____

_____

_____

_____

Why is that?

_____

_____

_____

At what age does your conscious mind start to be more fully developed?

_____

_____

_____

Relative to your goal, what are some beliefs that you want to start imprinting using Neurogenics?

_____

_____

_____

_____

Chapter 8

Superconscious Mind

In many ways the subconscious mind is much like the disk storage on a computer. It is used to store the programs and data that the computer needs to operate with. Your conscious mind is like the processor on the computer which retrieves the programs and data and processes them to operate your body.

An example of how the subconscious mind works is when we are driving a car long distance and became 'lost in our thoughts' only to find we are miles down the road without any conscious recall of the intervening countryside we have travelled through. Our subconscious mind carried on driving the car quite successfully during this time.

Another time might be when we unconsciously turn in the direction towards our workplace on our day off, when we consciously decided we wanted to go somewhere else. All these unconscious programs are of great benefit most of the time as they automatically help us to conduct our lives, leaving our conscious mind free to explore new thoughts. Unfortunately there are some unconscious or subconscious programs that are not beneficial to us and they can strongly work against us.

The Superconscious Mind

While the conscious and subconscious aspects of our mind are closely aligned with our physical shell or body, the superconscious mind is "beyond physical." Remember the functions of the conscious mind are to identify, reason and decide. The subconscious mind stores and retrieves information and obeys the commands of the conscious mind. The superconscious mind functions outside and beyond both of them, but is accessed through them.

In our example of a computer, the superconscious mind can be likened to the internet, which enables us to connect to every other computer in the world and the people using those computers. However with the superconscious connection we do not need any other technology other than what we are born with. Through the superconscious it is possible for us to connect to every other mind on the planet.

However, connecting to our superconscious opens up much wider doorways than just linking to other minds.

Now that you've been re-introduced to the individual aspects of mind, both the conscious mind and the subconscious mind, let's delve a little deeper and discover how and why these individual as well as the collective aspects of mind have the ability to tune into and harmonise with the "Super-Conscious" aspect of mind, and create the various events, conditions and circumstances in physical form that we call "reality." Once properly understood you'll have a greatly enhanced ability to begin attracting and manifesting desired results in your life intentionally and consistently...in EVERY aspect of your life. All personal greatness and individual achievement is based on it. In fact, everything we have discussed so far has been preparing you to use the powers of your Super-Conscious mind to transform all areas of your life.

Once you begin using your subconscious capabilities in a systematic way, you will get ideas from *out of the blue*. Almost everyone has had the experience of thinking of a good idea for a new product or service, but dismissed it, most likely because of a lack of confidence in their ability to take the idea to market. Months or years later someone makes a fortune from the very same idea. The difference between the person who had the idea and ignored it, and the person who acted on it, was the person who acted on it had a high level of trust and *belief* in themselves and their ability to turn that idea into reality.

Because of beliefs formed during childhood conditioning, we tend to ignore our own ideas, assuming that they could not be worth very much, when in fact they could change our entire lives.

Let's begin by taking a deeper look at the Super Conscious Mind and how this Super Conscious Mind determines our individual realities.

The Wonder and Awe Of The Super Conscious Mind

The Super-Conscious mind is the aspect of consciousness which is limitless or "Infinite" in nature and is called by many different names. Just a small sampling of these "man-made" labels are God, Supreme Energy, Source, Universe, Universal Intelligence, or Higher Power. Napoleon Hill referred to this power as "Infinite Intelligence."

Hill called it the universal storehouse of knowledge and the source of all imagination and creativity. He claimed that the ability to access this intelligence was a central part of the great success enjoyed by the hundreds of wealthy men and women he interviewed during twenty-five years of research into the book, "The Laws of Success," which was subsequently condensed into "Think And Grow Rich."

The scientific community refers to the Super-Conscious Mind as the "Quantum Universe" or in some cases "The Unified Field."

What you decide to call it is of no consequence. When any of these avenues are looked at, explored and studied from a deep perspective, the path inevitably leads back to the same Ultimate Source. For the sake of our description we'll refer to this Ultimate Source as Super Consciousness, or the Super-Conscious Mind.

This Super-Conscious Mind exists as an infinite field or matrix of potential which knows no boundaries or limitations. Within itself it contains EVERY probability, from the infinitely large to the infinitely small. It encompasses ALL things from the macroscopic to the microscopic and beyond. It comprises all things physical and those that are non-physical.

The Super Conscious Mind is all pervasive. It is within everything and exists everywhere. You could say that it is an Infinite Field of Potential without borders or restriction.

Within this "Infinite Field Of Potential" exists and is stored anything that has ever happened or been created in the past, everything which is currently being created, or whatever may be created at some point in the future. You could say that this Super Consciousness or Super-Conscious Mind is omniscient and omnipresent. It encompasses ALL things, all probabilities both the seen as well as the unseen.

Within this Infinite field of consciousness exists any and every conceivable outcome. From a strictly physical perspective, meaning the existence of anything that currently exists as "physical" which can be experienced with the limitations of the five physical senses. Within this Infinite field of possibility and potential exists the material things such as a garden shed, to multi-million pound mansions. Within it exists an old, oil burning scrap motor to a flame red 600 BHP Lamborghini. From rags to the finest linens in the world.

The Super Conscious Mind also consists of the "intangible" or things that are of a "spiritual nature."

The possibilities are literally "Infinite" in nature. There is nothing that doesn't already exist within it as a probability, meaning that if it can be idealised and conceptualised in mind, regardless of the perceived enormity, it does already exist as a probability and once conceptualised, the process which makes it "real" is initiated.

Whatever can be conceived in mind as an ideal and held as a focused and intentional thought and harmonised with action, will and must manifest itself in physical form REGARDLESS of what it might be. Whatever can be conceptualised in mind whether physical or otherwise already exists within the Super-Conscious mind as an already existing fact, and only requires the correct and consistent focus of consciousness whether individually or collectively to make it a physical reality.

Now the Super-Conscious mind also consists of you, your family, your neighbours, your friends, everyone. Since this Super-Conscious mind is the "ALL in ALL" of everything conceivable, to fully grasp what it is, it's necessary to understand that ALL things whether seen or unseen broken down into their most basic and purest form are at their core comprised of pure energy. Since this Super-Conscious Mind and everything within it are made of this same stuff...this means YOU as well.

Put more simply, your individual ability to think, feel and act in ways that YOU choose individually, is what determines precisely what you are choosing to draw from the Super-Conscious Mind. It's this choice that determines each of the events, conditions and circumstances in your life that collectively make up your life experience.

So, how do you make this choice? Through your individual consciousness. More specifically, the quality of your dominant method of thinking and how you perceive reality.

When you become consciously aware of those choices, you begin to see and understand that it is your individual "being-ness" that determines what is drawn from the Super-Conscious Mind and what is experienced in your life as "physical things."

Regardless of what you may observe in a physical sense with the limitations of the five physical senses of sight, hearing, touch, taste, and smell, through digging a little deeper and giving some thought to where each of these "physical things" were derived from, you'll discover that each and every thing that has existed, or ever will exist began with and happened as a result of an initially held thought or ideal.

It all exists as the result of Consciousness.

Until a thought or ideal was produced or conceived in the mind, the possibility of this "things" physical existence would be impossible. Since EVERYTHING both seen and unseen already exists within the Super-Conscious Mind, until conceived it would still exist only as a probability in the unseen or spiritual realm of the Super-Conscious Mind as a "Probability" of existence.

Although this may be a bit difficult to comprehend, let's look at everyday physical objects that you use today so that you can fully grasp the reality of just how true this is and why due to your individual right to choose, combined with the existence of the Super-Conscious mind, you have been provided with the ability to both create and experience whatever you choose and are able to conceive it as a reality.

It will soon become clear as to how you have the ability to experience a kind and quality of life that few people understand. Hopefully you'll begin to fully recognise and acknowledge the limitless power provided to you, to be, do and have whatever you it is you choose.

The Super Conscious Mind and Henry Ford

Get an image of the car you drive...

Where did it come from? It came from the showroom right? Go back further. The factory? Go back further. The design team? Eventually, you will always end up at the mind. Where did the factory come from? Where did the parts which make up the car come from? Where did the bricks that made the factory "real" come from? Where did the machinery that builds the cars come from?

Someone had to "think them" ALL into reality.

Although you see them in physical form, prior to them being manufactured or even conceived as an ideal, they must have existed somewhere right?

Let's use a specific example...

Think back to the time before Henry Ford created and developed the world's first low-priced, cast-in-one-piece V-8 engine. Prior to its creation and development, it wasn't yet "real"...meaning it wasn't yet a "physical reality." It existed only in Henry Ford's mind as a thought, an ideal or conceptualisation which prior to being created existed only as a "probability of existence."

The engineers and designers of that time attempted to convince Henry Ford that they couldn't DO what he had conceptualised and envisioned them doing. For them it wasn't possible to create this "thing." Yet Henry Ford chose to persist and kind of like the modern day Nike commercial told them to, "Just do it!"

He knew it could be done even as far from "reality" as those who were attempting to design and create it "perceived it" as being. It wasn't yet real, yet at the same time it did already exist somewhere.

Where was that?

Within the Super-Conscious mind or if you prefer, the Infinite Field of Potential.

The car couldn't possibly exist until someone, in this case Henry Ford, had the imagination or what might be referred to as a vision...a heightened level of consciousness to think that it could be a physical reality. Until the ideal was established in the mind of Henry Ford, the reality of using and benefiting from this new design of engine existed only as a probability of existence.

It wasn't yet a "reality."

When thought of, held in the mind and conceived as a possibility, it then became a theory. This theory, which through aligning correct thoughts, emotions and actions with it, enabled it to manifest and become a "fact" in the physical world.

This concept then explains what steel industrialist and richest man on the planet, Andrew Carnegie was trying to explain to us.

"Any idea that is held in the mind, that is emphasised, that is either feared or revered, will begin at once to cloth itself in the most convenient and appropriate form available."
– Andrew Carnegie

The original individually held quality of consciousness of Henry Ford was transmuted from "pure consciousness" to thought, resulting in an ideal or conceptualisation, resulting in action which led to the creation of his automobile. The originally held thought or ideal was conceived and derived from the unseen or spiritual realm.

What is this place? The Infinite Field of Potential...The Super-Conscious mind.

Pretty cool stuff when you really think about it.

But it's NOT just limited to cars, engines and Henry Ford.

It's exactly the same with *anything* that you can think of that currently exists in the world. Whether it's mobile phones, Lear Jets, satellite navigation, aftershave, the book that you're reading right now, Rolex watches, beach umbrellas, the clothes you're wearing, the use of the internet......EVERYTHING!

ALL of them began from somewhere. They weren't just "not here," and then all of a sudden just showed up! They were all derived from "somewhere." This somewhere was in the mind of those who have been credited with their creation which drew this originally held thought, ideal or conceptualisation from this Infinite Field Of Potential, the Super-Conscious mind.

Each of these modern day inventions began and were made "real" as a result of individual consciousness. They were made possible as the result of the individual laws of mind, beginning as a thought, which was broadcast as a frequency of energy and sent into the Infinite Field Of Potential.

It's these individual Laws, that govern the force of all of creation. Laws such as the Law of Vibration, combined with the unwavering certainty of the Law of Attraction, and the outcomes determined by The Law of Perpetual Transmutation of Energy, which eventually resulted in the manifestation of the thing thought of, conceptualised and idealised.

It's these processes that enables ALL things that are "unseen and intangible" to become "seen and tangible."

You, your consciousness, EVERYTHING exists as energy, and you have been provided the ability to consciously direct that energy to create (co-create) your reality based on the kind and quality of consciousness that you choose to project through your thoughts, ideals and conceptualisations.

Regardless of what they might be, they DO already exist as a probability in this field...this Super-Conscious Mind. It's simply a matter of you choosing to consciously create and intentionally conceptualise them.

OK, now that we've established that as fact, since everything that exists originated from a thought, or an ideal, it becomes clear that those things which exist or ever have existed in your business or personal life as well as those that you will experience in the future, are also the result of the quality of consciousness or thought as well.

It doesn't matter how or even whether you perceive them as good or bad, joyful or painful etc. Each is just a result of what you think and *believe* that it will be. It's what you choose to interpret, conceptualise and "think about" most often that makes them real and right and true for you.

Understand this. Think about the "Infinite" possibilities available to YOU!!! If you can conceive it in mind... WHATEVER it is, you can draw it from this Infinite Field of Potential, the Super-Conscious Mind. There is no limit to this power.

Now that's REALLY cool don't you think?

Next, let's look at some of the mechanics behind why this is true and take a more practical look at why it is true as well as how and why it works the way it does.

The Super Conscious Mind and The Unwavering Process Which Makes Things "Real"

According to the Law of Vibration, everything, including thought or consciousness exists as a vibrational frequency which, regardless of the intensity of the frequency is broadcast into the Super-Conscious, or the Infinite Field Of Potential. It attracts to itself additional energies of a harmonious frequency and through the process of manifestation (The Law Of Perpetual Transmutation) produces physical results that you can see, feel, touch, taste and smell in your life.

The Super-Conscious makes no distinctions, determinations or judgments as to what you choose to project into it or draw from it but rather, as ancient spiritual text states, the Super-Conscious Mind provides "Whatsoever ye desire."

This is where so many have a difficult time believing or grasping this because most AREN'T experiencing everything they desire.

Well...there's also a practical and logical explanation as to why.

Although many may have had a conscious desire to experience something, it isn't the *conscious* aspect of mind which is responsible for communicating and connecting with the Super-Conscious. It's the *subconscious* aspect of mind that acts as the communication and broadcasting device with the Super-Conscious, and based on what's programmed at this subconscious level, determines your physical results.

Your desires, which are determined by your conscious thought patterns, either harmonise with or conflict with core beliefs stored in the subconscious aspects of your mind. These beliefs determine which frequency you are broadcasting into this Super-Conscious "infinite" field of potential.

If you have a conscious desire to have more money, but at a subconscious level think you're going to be broke based on previously created beliefs established around you and money, you are in essence broadcasting an energy that is not in resonance with creating the "reality" of money in your life.

Rather than consistently thinking the thoughts about being abundant in the area of money, and the emotions being created as a result of these thoughts about money, the message or "asking" is of lack and limitation. This resonance of lack and limitation which is being projected into the Super-Conscious...where ALL possibilities exist, are projected due to your subconscious beliefs about money, wealth and abundance. You will and DO attract to you precisely what you are asking for.

Although you may have a strong desire to have this money or whatever else the conscious desire might be, it's the underlying and often unconscious beliefs you hold that determine and CAUSE the various events, conditions and circumstances in your life.

It's your "resonance" that is creating your reality. It's this RESONANCE that determines what you are asking the Super-Conscious Mind to deliver to you. This resonance serves as the communication device with the Super-Conscious Mind.

With that being true...

There's another extremely important distinction to make with regard to all this resonance and asking stuff...

That is...

Make A Conscious and Consistent Effort To Focus On What You Want...NOT On What You DON'T Want!

If you place conscious focus on NOT being broke you are still in essence placing focus on the opposite of that which is desired. This will draw from this Super-Consciousness, the thing or result that the predominant focus remains fixated upon, which in this case is being broke.

The only possibility to change the outcome is to change the vibrational resonance of the thought. Rather than focusing on NOT being broke, the predominant focus should remain fixated on having an abundant amount of money, internalising it as an already existing reality, igniting the emotions that are responsible for intensifying the energy broadcast into the "Infinite Field of Potential" and the result is that you will draw from the Super-Conscious Mind, the people, resources and materials needed to create the desired result.

You can never create a desired outcome by placing your predominant focus on the absence of its polar opposite. If you desire monetary wealth it is necessary to keep thoughts focused on the attainment of monetary wealth NOT the lack of or absence of lack.

The subconscious patterns (beliefs) that you have established throughout your life are the determining factor as to what you are asking the Super-Conscious Mind to provide you with. Subconscious patterns that are based on lack and limitation are the determining factor as to what limitations you are experiencing and are strictly due to the limiting beliefs you hold in your subconscious mind.

Judge Judy

Contrary to what many believe to be true, there is no judgment as to what will or will not be received nor is there such a thing that so many perceive and refer to as "unanswered prayer." When a desire is expressed in the way that most have been taught, which is a physical form of communication, if the underlying beliefs aren't in alignment with the "verbal" asking and the manifestation doesn't occur, it is due to a subconscious process, a core belief which is keeping the desired outcome from you, NOT the denial of the Super-Conscious Mind to provide it.

The Super-Conscious Mind doesn't say yes to some things and no to others.

If it appears that your desired outcome isn't being manifest, it isn't because the Super Conscious Mind is vetoing your request. It is ONLY because you don't "BELIEVE" that it will. Through conscious observation we can understand and feel a disharmony between the conscious and subconscious aspects of our minds. In other words there exists a "subconscious belief" that is keeping the desired outcome from becoming a physical reality.

The Super Conscious Mind ALWAYS says YES!

Next, let's look at how and why it works this way.....

I'm going to ask that you visualise yourself inside a spaceship and send yourself out of the earth's atmosphere, thousands of miles into space, eventually landing on the moon. BUT... before you get into this spaceship take a good look around you and observe all the things in your surroundings whatever they might be. The possibilities are infinite as to what that might be.

You may be sitting in your lounge, and see a table, a TV that it's sitting on, a clock and some family photographs. Now step outside of your home and walk about 50 yards, turn around and face your house. These things that you were looking at in the individual room are no longer visible to you correct? Although you know they still exist they are invisible to you but you know they are still in the house. Ok, now it's time to step into your space ship and blast off.

When you land on the moon shut off the engine and look out the window. What do you see? Can you see your house? No. Can you see the roads that lead to your house. No. Can you see the launching pad from where you blasted off from? No. So, what can you see? Chances are you see the Earth as a HUGE big ball with blue, green and brown colours that resembles a large marble.

Can you see any movement or activity on top of this big marble? No. But before you blasted off you were able to see all the individual objects that existed there prior, correct? The cars, the houses, the fields, the stores, all the activity which was going on. Now allow your mind to envision these things again. Although you can't see them from your current vantage point you can envision them. These things represent the organisms that exist within the macroscopic.

Next take a look at your hand. It appears solid doesn't it? Maybe, if you're like most, you think it is solid. Although it appears solid based on what you can see with the naked eye, if you were to place it under a powerful microscope you would find that it's not solid at all. It's made up of organisms as well. In fact there are MANY microscopic forms of life existing in and on your body that you aren't aware of and are unable to comprehend because of the limitations of your physical senses.

The point being is that you exist as an individual being...as an organism in comparison to the Infinite and vast Universe that we exist in. BUT...being created in "The Image and Likeness" of Source...this Super Conscious Mind, you are an extremely important and integral part of this infinite vastness. You have been provided the ability (through your mental faculties) as well as the power, to draw whatever exists within this field of Infinite Potential to and through you.

Transmuting The Mystical Nature Of The Super Conscious Mind Into Practical, Physical and Tangible Results

We've covered A LOT of ground. Here's the bottom line...

Everything is a result of consciousness. That which is not yet here in physical form, which has not yet been discovered and conceived in mind exists within this Infinite Field Of Potentiality. The Super-Conscious Mind IS that field.

You only need think it into being, hold it in mind as an already existing reality in the physical world and the ways and actions needed to bring it into your reality will manifest just as you instruct.

Based on the spiritual teachings of the greatest, wisest and most insightful teachers in the history of the world, you have the ability as well as the free will to create "whatsoever ye desire," the limitations of which are based only on what you believe is possible for yourself.

According to modern day science for every cause there is an effect, the kind and quality of which is determined only by the cause which created it. Thoughts are causes, conditions are effects.

You and your beliefs serve as the cause and the effect experienced. As a result what are the effects of these beliefs on your behaviour?

Everything.

When observing nature it is apparent that whatever seed you plant, you will receive a harvest based on and limited to the type of seed planted.

You can choose what each and every area of your life will consist of once you learn to become consciously aware that ALL things are possible, that you as an integral part of the whole have the ability to make them a reality, to develop a conscious awareness of the seeds that you are planting through your thought process.

By consciously, purposefully and intentionally holding the desired outcome as an already existing fact, aligning and allowing your emotions to ignite as if you already possessed it as an already existing physical reality, the Super-Conscious Mind will deliver it to you without judgment, just as you instruct, believe and expect to experience.

You have been provided an inalienable right of free will to think as you choose to think. You have the ability to consciously control those emotions which act as the "frequency intensifier" of those thoughts and conceptualisations that you choose to think. You hold the same identical ability to create a life that you choose regardless of what you might currently observe, believe and perceive reality to be.

You can choose to begin consciously and purposefully creating whatsoever "desired" results that you choose to experience in your life or choose to remain an unconscious creator fully believing that whatever you experience in life happens as the result of some random and uncontrollable set of capricious external circumstances or luck!

Whichever you choose is your right. Whatever you believe is "Absolutely Correct." There is no right or wrong reality. There is however, "Higher Truth" which will enable you to experience a higher quality of life that the majority only dream about. Once you become aware of your individual power to create and become empowered to use and believe in its manifestation, your life will never be the same again.

Whatever the mind can conceive and believe it will achieve.

All that we are, all that exists in the entire cosmos is made up of this same stuff. Pure energy. Your individual consciousness is energy. The limitless and infinite potential which exists within the Super-Conscious Mind is energy.

Become conscious of that simple fact, develop an unshakable "knowingness" regarding who and what you truly are, consciously and purposefully constructing your thoughts based on "Infinite Potentiality," clearly defining your desired outcomes and you will achieve self-mastery to create and experience the life of your dreams without limit.

You have been designed with the mental faculties as well as the free will to discover and consciously harmonise with this Super-Conscious mind to begin consciously creating a life that very few are aware of. The rewards received for making that conscious choice will be fulfilment, joy, purpose, peace and limitless abundance in each and every area of your life.

"As you believe so shall you receive."

Superconscious Exercises

There are several ways to activate superconscious activity. The first and most dependable is to simply think about your goal all the time. Because the conscious mind can only hold one image in the mind at one time, this alone will keep you focused and happy. It will force superconscious activities to flow through you in the form of ideas and inspiration towards goal attainment. It sets up a "tension" between your conscious mind and the superconscious mind like a salivating dog waiting impatiently for you to throw it a ball. As soon as you release the ball from your hand, the dog immediately scampers off to fetch the ball back to you. Your superconscious works in a similar way, and as such you must release your goal in order for the superconscious to help you.

The second way to stimulate your superconscious is through meditation or solitude. It provides an opportunity to reflect on who you are and what's important to you. Most importantly though it causes superconscious solutions to spring into your mind full-blown and complete. If you've never done it before get ready for a real experience.

In today's world we are bombarded with outside information that is a real distraction. This inhibits our mental power to perform at our best. This is the absolute best way to begin to "create your own reality" and distinguish the things you really want from the current reality. Practice blocking out 20-30 minutes daily to concentrate solely on your goal and you will see and attract possibilities that just weren't available to you before. If you focus continually on the goal most important to you, the subconscious mind accepts this goal as a command and is eventually passed on to your superconscious mind for realisation.

A superconscious solution has three characteristics. First of all when it comes, it is always within your resources and capabilities at the time. It is always simple and fairly easy to implement. Second, it appears as a "BFO," or a blinding flash of the obvious. You wonder why you hadn't thought of it before. And of course the reason why you hadn't thought of it before is because you haven't asked before!

The third way you can tell if you've got a superconscious solution is that it comes with a sudden burst of elation. A feeling that makes you want to take action on it straight away. Sometimes you'll not be able to sleep as you'll be mulling over all the great things that you'll be able to do as a consequence of implementing what you've been guided to do.

When you have a clear goal, a plan backed by the real belief that it can happen, you activate your superconscious mind to bring you whatever you need to make it a reality. When you really believe in something, you will be led to do and say the right thing at the right time in every situation. You bring yourself into complete alignment with the greatest power in the universe.

EXERCISES

Think of any man made, real tangible product.

Maybe a house, hotel, airport, car, whatever.

Work backwards from the most tangible level and you will find that nothing happens until thought starts the process in action at the level of consciousness.

Your results don't just happen. You think into them.

Notes:

_____

_____

_____

_____

Chapter 9

MSI MASTERMINDING

The great achievements of your life-first built as mind concepts, then made real are not just limited to the power of your own mind. A myriad of other minds can tune in and give you their thoughts by concentrating on your goal and implementing superconscious activity on your behalf to bring you some incredible ideas. All big ideas are the result of a multiplicity of minds working together harmoniously.

This quote by Napoleon Hill (given to him by Andrew Carnegie) opened my mind dramatically once I finally got it.

"No individual may have great power without availing himself of the "Master Mind." "The accumulation of great fortunes calls for power, and power is acquired through highly organised, intelligently directed, specific knowledge. But that knowledge does not necessarily have to be in the possession of the person who accumulates the fortune."
— Napoleon Hill

If you are a business owner and you want to increase your revenue and find innovative ideas for your business, you need a mastermind!

The What and Why of Masterminding

You've heard about it and seen the results successful business owners are achieving, but do you really know what a Mastermind is?

In short, a mastermind is two or more people who come together to help each other, to share their ideas, skills and knowledge to increase business revenue, create innovative solutions for complex business challenges and form an alliance of minds to be the very best they can be!

Why Masterminding is Essential for Business and Personal Growth

Masterminding is not a new idea, or the most recent business growth quick fix. Masterminding was first introduced to the masses by Napoleon Hill, who said "No two minds ever come together without thereby creating a third, invisible intangible force, which may be likened to a third mind." The most successful business owners, either now or in the past, have been involved in a mastermind group. Think Henry Ford, Thomas Edison, and even Walt Disney, all of whom have belonged to a mastermind group and have achieved enormous success.

How a Mastermind Can Significantly Improve Your Business

It can be lonely at the top, and recent studies have shown that our brains work better when collaborating in groups versus relying solely on ourselves. Working in a group allows for the "third mind," this greater intelligence, to expand what is possible. Wouldn't it be great to have a group of people with opposing strengths that complement one another? One of the key benefits in forming a mastermind group is having a support system in place with people who have a diverse skill set, unique experiences, and a desire to be the best. Also, a mastermind group provides a medium for you to share your unique skills and knowledge to reinforce what you know. Furthermore, you have instant accountability, and we all know that we are 90% more likely to achieve our goals when we have to answer to someone else!

Making instant contacts and connections with other business owners is one of the many bonuses of a mastermind group.

Back in 1993 a study was conducted at Brigham Young University related to goal achievement. The study found that the probability of achieving a particular goal was associated with the statements a person made about the goal.

- People who said "That's a good idea" had a 10% chance.

- Those who said "I'll do it," had a 25% chance of reaching their goal.

- Those who put a date by which they planned to achieve their goal had a 40% chance of doing so.

- Those who developed a specific plan for reaching their goal had a 50% chance of getting there.

- Those who committed to someone else that they would accomplish their goal had a 60% chance of making it.

- But those people who committed to someone else and also committed to share their progress at regular intervals had a 95% chance of reaching their goal!!

The power of accountability is incredible and, as you can see, greatly increases your chances of doing what you say you are going to do. This is one reason why it is so important to have a coach or a mentor. How many times have you made a commitment to yourself, but then let yourself off the hook when the going gets tough. It is next to impossible for you to see past your own logic! Finding an accountability partner can be one of the most powerful things you can ever do if you REALLY want to reach a particular goal.

Finding the right accountability partner is critical. It should be someone you can trust with your dreams and someone whose opinion you value and for whom you have great respect (in other words it would hurt to let them down). In some cases it could be a best friend or a spouse (sometimes, however, those people could be the very WORST accountability partners) a business colleague, a networking associate, etc. You have to be willing to commit to what you wish to be held accountable for, to sharing your progress at regular intervals and they have to be willing to hold your feet to the fire and carry through with the consequence if need be. Your Accountability Partner must agree to request progress reports from you at an agreed upon interval of time.

If left to you to provide these updates, you would likely forget all about them – this is your minds paradigm's way of sabotaging you, insuring that you stay right where you are.

Accountability without consequence is meaningless. Some may say, "Well, the consequence for not meeting my deadline is that I don't reach my goal," and that's true, but as human beings we are pleasure seekers and pain avoiders. It is my experience that accountability contracts that have a clearly defined consequence for non-performance work best. The consequence needs to be a source of more pain than the tasks associated with what you're being held accountable for. Threatening to take peoples cars if they don't do what they say they will, works well for me!

Being involved in a mastermind group can not only help you in creating newer, faster much more profitable ideas, but more importantly it can stop you from wasting your time and making the wrong decisions. Often, years and years can go by doing the same thing day in day out, not getting the results you want and then one day Bam! You make the decision to join a Mastermind group and everything starts to change. I've seen it happen time and time again.

On Your Own Jack

Imagine being given an idea that could possibly save you 5, 10 or 20 years of business building toil by casually conversing with a group of other motivated individuals.

How long have you been trying to create the freedom you want on your own? You can spend an entire life building a network of associates and peers who will never, ever operate at your level. You can't pull them up; they can't help you rise any further. In the end they only pull you down.

In contrast a good Mastermind group attracts only the highest-minded innovators who, working together create a safe and inspiring environment that nourishes and encourages the growth of your minds most powerful concepts. As you work together, you'll create that "third mind" that propels your dreams into realities.

If I work on a goal or challenge by myself, I have a certain degree of creative power to solve what needs solving. If I then ask you to join me and apply your mind-power to work on my goal or challenge, then we feel there is more than just the power of the two of us, now it's like the Mastermind takes over. It's no longer two, it's more like the power of eleven! When you take a burning candle and touch the flame of another candle, the focused power of the two together is so much brighter than the two operating individually.

X Factor

Most of us live our lives without knowing about the conditioning that governs our lives. I call this conditioning the X Factor. It's very important to understand how your conditioning affects your thinking.

In order to win, you have to break away from the masses unless you are happy getting the same results they are.

The X Factor can be any ingrained pattern of belief or behaviour, from what weight you think you should be, to how you run a business, to the way you are with people. Let's say that maybe X is the idea that you can't earn more than £30,000 a year. If you go to wealth creation seminars maybe you come away thinking that what you really want to earn is £200,000 a year. This new idea is the Y Factor. Now the war is on!

You'll no doubt play with the idea in your conscious mind at first, possibly visualizing your new, wealthy life. The X factor plays with your mind and tries to convince you that it's just a pipe dream. It's not really going to work, at least not for you. Your internal self-talk kicks in with, "Well, I don't really want to work that hard, I'm doing Ok really, I don't want to risk what I've already got. What if it doesn't work out?" Now you're screwed. You not only have no *external* support in the form of a coach or group to encourage and support you through this growth period, but you have to deal with your *internal* negative B.S. as well.

Every time you visualise a good reason why this will work, X will offer a rational, logical sensible reason why it won't. This is why persistence is needed to combat this old conditioning. You have little chance against X unless you can alter your belief system and get support along the way.

Origins

People have used Masterminding throughout history to solve life's problems. It's been said that Jesus and his twelve disciples were one of the first recorded in history! As far back as you can go, people have been involved in working out problems through sitting down, discussing the scope of what needs to be done and joining together in a spirit of harmony, where the sole objective is to help the person discover new and improved ways of doing things. Ways that would make something easier, more profitable, more scalable and more fun.

It's like joining several batteries together and watching the power of all of them create more power than the total energy they could bring individually. What happens is often truly amazing.

A mastermind group is not a social gathering of friends, neither is it a session to air your gripes about life and get a cuddle. To make a Mastermind work, it has to be made up of people who are positive, self-motivated and proactive and who have a desire to help each other reach their goals.

Effective Masterminding

Having facilitated Masterminds nationally in a physical capacity and internationally by skype or on a call, I have found that certain, but very important criteria are essential if it is to return the maximum benefits. Without these key strategies the groups tend to fizzle out.

Select DOERS not TALKERS!

As you know, the people you associate with has a huge effect on your mind and ultimately your success. They WILL influence you. Be certain that the people you associate with have similar values and aspirations.

It is of little value to be in a group of people who talk about what needs to be done or things they could do, but not take action on them. This creates inertia and reinforces your feeling of still being stuck. You need an environment of energy and expectation.

Ensure that people have a track record of results, that they actually do what they say they will do-and not just talk about it. If it's just the company that you're after, then go get a Labrador!

Select Stingers, Not Leeches

In the insect world, a stinger confronts and attacks by striking, whereas a leech sucks its victim dry.

In Mastermind groups (and 121 coaching) it is much better to have stingers. These are people who offer honest, upfront, and direct feedback on your work by giving you information and insight that is of value, with no hidden agenda. It might sting a bit at times, but far better to hear it now than years down the line when you've wasted a whole load of time and money. On the other hand, leeches are takers. They sit and suck in information and advice from others, offering very little value to the group. It's a mindset thing. They believe you have to go out and get without giving first. They put the cart before the horse. They haven't yet learnt that the more you give the more you get in return. Leeches are often overfriendly-until they get what they want and then drop you like a hot spud. Be careful...

Select Chiefs Not Indians

Chiefs take the bull by the horns, they set goals and action plans and inspire others to step up a level and become all they can be. They believe in themselves and push others to do the same. They are forward focused and spend little time, if any, worrying about the past or wallowing in their mistakes.

Indians don't lead, they follow the herd. They don't express their opinion unless asked. They have to be encouraged to try new things and often resist change. They drag back the progress of the others in the group because they are waiting for someone to give them the answer instead of being proactive in finding it themselves.

MSI Magic

A lot of entrepreneurs are interested in time freedom. They want to spend their time doing what they love, whether they get paid for it or not.

Not surprisingly, wealthy people who have time freedom do things differently. They find a better way and then multiply it. When I write a book for example it gets resold in physical form at events or bought online through the internet. I don't always have to be there for someone to buy the thing. I do the work once and leverage that work many times over in order to create more time freedom. In addition to this I gain income from it as well. But it also provides a vehicle to reach and help more people. Wealthy people have all usually chosen the Multiple Sources of Income route-the MSI route.

Your PSI-primary source of income is your job, and if it's not systemised properly that could mean your business as well. You really want to get passive income flowing to you from various sources.

For example, if you are in financial services you could create additional income from this business by giving seminars, training others, creating information products in the form of books, audio programs or online memberships of some kind. Most people in business are really looking for financial freedom and emotional well-being. Creating MSI's are a great way to achieve this.

MSI Technology

"Multiple sources of income is a technology which will permit you to multiply your income by providing service beyond that which you are presently providing at your primary source of income."

ADDITIONAL SERVICE – ADDITIONAL INCOME

Way back in the 1960's it only took one source of income for a family to survive, today very few families can survive on less than two, and even that won't be enough in the future. You'd be wise to create multiple sources.

The Right Way to Create Multiple Streams of Residual Income

If you are going to pursue multiple sources of income then it is important to follow a proven, step-by-step process that will maximise your odds of success. Below is that step-by-step process:

Step 1: Master the First Stream of Income

Begin by picking one stream of income that you are deeply passionate about and know a fair amount about. For some people it will be the property game and for others it will be owning your own business or share trading for example.

Your first stream of income should be something so personally exciting that you would do it whether you ever made money at it or not, just to learn the process.

Why? Because the first stream of income will be the toughest.

This is where you will develop your Mastermind team members, learn fundamental skills applicable to all streams of income, overcome personal obstacles to success and create enough cash flow to get you out of the rat race of only swapping your time for money.

Your first stream of residual income is where you will get the most bumps and bruises. By choosing an area you are passionate about it will increase the odds that you persist long enough to clear all the hurdles and succeed.

Master your first stream of income and in the process you will develop the necessary talents and abilities that can then be leveraged to develop other streams of income.

Step 2: Systematise the First Stream of Income

Once you have mastered the first stream of income then it is time to systematise that stream so that it no longer requires your limited time and attention.

Systematising is done through the application of time leverage and technology leverage, usually humans and the internet. Master the skills of systematising so that your first success runs on auto-pilot without requiring a lot of your time thus earning you residual income and cash flow.

Step 3: Leverage Resources to Create Additional Streams of Residual Income

Once you have systematised the first stream of income to produce residual income without your involvement, then you have the free time and energy to add multiple streams of income.

This is done by *intelligently adding additional revenue streams that leverage the skills, knowledge, and network you created in the first stream of income so that you aren't starting from scratch on each additional stream.* This is a key point.

For example, I know of highly successful direct marketers who have leveraged their marketing skills, network, and databases to create residual income through offering other product lines with minimal effort to the same market.

Another example is Robert Kiyosaki, bestselling author of "Rich Dad Poor Dad," who got out of the rat race through property. Then he added paper assets and leveraged the financial knowledge he gained from his investment business experience in property into a successful information publishing business.

Notice the pattern. *Each of the above successful examples developed multiple streams of income by learning the base skills in one stream and then leveraging those skills later to create additional streams.*

Each successful example learns to walk with one stream before running with multiple streams of residual income.

I challenge you to examine anyone who has succeeded with multiple streams of income and see if they violated the rules of walking before running. Every "multiple streamer" I have ever met built their success from one stream they were passionate about first.

Only after that initial success with one stream of income did they leverage their resources into multiple streams of income.

In fact, to do it any other way is to throw away one of the primary benefits of multiple streams of income: leverage of existing resources.

It takes less effort to operate each additional stream of income because they are all built upon the same foundational resources.

When you attempt to create multiple streams of income simultaneously, you'll create mayhem and confusion instead of leverage because no base resources exist to build upon. It makes no sense. It has no advantage sufficient to justify the problems it creates. From a mind-set point of view it becomes really confusing because your mental efforts are also diffused as well. Man who aims at both rabbits, hits neither.

The bottom line is if you are going to build multiple streams of income, then there is a right and wrong way to go about it.

Following this step-by-step process will help you maximise your odds of success. Here are some criteria to help you when you're considering a multiple source of income for yourself.

This is only a general guideline. I recommend you follow it closely until you have learned the process of developing MSI's.

Some or all of these should be part of your MSI development. Do not worry if your idea requires you to go against this list.

YOUR MULTIPLE SOURCE OF INCOME SHOULD...

1. Be low-risk.

I recommend the first few projects remain in the low-risk category. Work on ideas that have a greater chance of success. Take it on a project-by-project basis.

2. Have low time involvement.

One of your first considerations should be the time involvement. I have found if your MSI takes you away from your PSI (Primary Source of Income) and the returns are not immediate, then people tend to give up on the MSI before it has had time to mature and prosper. The intention is for you to work on generating MSI's on a part-time basis for the time being.

Most of us grew up with the belief that "hard work," which often translated to "long hours," was a prerequisite to success.

3. Low Management

Since this is not our main occupation, I suggest developing new ideas that fall under the category of low management. If your plans are too elaborate the idea will probably die on the vine.

4. Demand only low personal energy.

If you are too taxed by your MSI you will not stick with it. This is what our experience shows. Yes, it will demand some of your energy; but during the learning phase, either work only with ideas that require low personal energy or have others involved with you to share the workload.

5. Require low investment.

Wealthy people become wealthy using the first rule of entrepreneurship: "OPM=Other People's Money." Make good use of this rule. A warning: Get your feet wet first though before you use OPM or your own. Learn how to get several MSI's first, and then you will be able to acquire capital once and if it is needed.

Also, this doesn't mean that if a great opportunity came your way you shouldn't put up your own money. At times we have all had to do this to start a new venture. Just be careful if this is your first MSI.

6. Require higher level thinking.

Your MSI's should involve ideas, not labour. It is much more profitable working with information or ideas than shovels and hammers. Not that there is anything wrong with these things, but the person who deals in ideas is always the highest paid.

7. Produce high return.

This is one criteria upon which I always insist. It is a must. Wealthy people do not play with small ideas. Be sure there are healthy profits in any MSI you consider. You need to factor in all expenses and other costs before you can determine the return potential. There are a million ways to earn a million-but some are easier than others.

8. Deliver high service.

Any business or Multiple Source of Income which focuses on customer needs will do well. I have long said that any business which helps busy people save time will be very successful in our society. Be sure your MSI provides a real service to the customer. Put the needs of the customer and their problems first before you think of the cash.

9. Reward yourself with high personal satisfaction.

Your MSI's should be personally satisfying. You will soon discover money alone will rarely satisfy. You could and should be enjoying your life. I would never do anything that didn't provide me with a healthy degree of internal or emotional satisfaction. This doesn't mean there aren't parts of your MSI you do not enjoy performing or completing; everyone will have some of that. In other words, don't select an MSI dealing with children if you don't like children.

There are ideas and cash potential for anyone who is awake enough to find MSI's in exactly the field of their dreams.

10. Contain high growth or education factors.

The purpose, in addition to creating additional sources of income, is for you to grow. This will happen automatically by virtue of your first effort. Once you have created your first MSI, you will know it CAN be done, and you will know HOW to do it.

The purpose of mastering money is not for the money itself, but for the raising of your consciousness; and by understanding that you have been operating from false concepts about the generation of income. You will find that you can have MULTIPLE sources of income and it won't cost you your marriage, your health or your life. You did it and you feel great. You grew in your awareness of the great potential within you.

Contact Me

If you have a hard time coming up with a viable MSI for yourself or are looking to join a Mastermind to help you with it, simply email me and I will be able to help you come up with a few ideas or put you in touch with the right people to get you started in your area.

The Possibilities

Each of us has more talents and capabilities than we realise, and we do ourselves a disservice when we place limitations on the possibilities. If you can think of a dozen things you can do for fun, you'll never get bored. If you can think of a dozen ways to earn money, you'll never be broke. And if you can think of a dozen reasons why you will succeed, you'll never be intimidated by temporary setbacks. Try it.

The Fun Dozen: Think of twelve things that you can do for fun any time you experience them.

The Earning Dozen: Think of twelve ways you can earn money.

The Success Dozen: Think of twelve reasons why you WILL succeed.

See if you can make the connection between some of the items on your completed lists in each of these three categories.

POTENTIAL MSI's

✓ Franchising

✓ Licensing

✓ Provide done for you marketing materials to specific industries

✓ Software development for lagging markets

✓ Create a *duplicatable* newsletter for specific industries

✓ Start a speciality school: Cooking/Business/Car Repairs for Women

✓ Give Speeches

✓ Write a book

✓ Create Cd's on your topic

✓ Import ideas that work in other countries

✓ Split up land and sell it in individual plots at a higher price

✓ Import from China and sell on Amazon

✓ Become a consultant

✓ Start a retreat center

✓ Run an online business

✓ Sell artwork online

✓ Write an advice column for the newspaper

✓ Network marketing

✓ Recycling waste

✓ Find underutilised assets in small businesses

✓ Manufacture your own products and white label them

✓ Get the re-sell rights for products from other countries

Narrow the List

Come up with a short list of five potential MSI's. You should select the five by asking this question, "Of all these ideas, which five excite me most?"

Now just pick one from the five. Select the one idea which you will begin developing until you learn the process of creating MSI's. This should be an idea which you will start working on NOW.

Mastermind this MSI

Lay out your MSI idea with the other members of your Mastermind team. See if it fits all the ten criteria mentioned previously to help you get off to a flying start. As mentioned before the best starts are had by those people that already have some level of experience with the market they intend to go into. Go on then, get on with it!

EXERCISES

Why is a Mastermind a great idea?

_____

_____

_____

_____

Who do you know that would be great Mastermind participants?

_____

_____

_____

_____

What would your group all have in common?

_____

_____

_____

_____

Chapter 10

Get On With It!

After many years of research, all the great scientists, researchers and psychologists remind us time and time again that having a purpose is the number one prerequisite to happiness, productivity and self-fulfillment. The lack of a definitive purpose or goal is the number one reason for failure, unhappiness and lack of self-motivation. If you don't have an image in your mind of the outcome or goal that you want (hopefully positive) by law, your mind will fill that "gap" with anything that isn't the outcome that you want, probably negative. This negative image attracts other similar and like thoughts and images to it, creating a perpetual cycle of negativity. This is really difficult to break, unless you are aware that it is you that is creating this in the first place!

The Magpie Effect

You can only hold one image in the mind at one time. Put simply you are either thinking about what you want or you aren't. The unwanted feelings of ambivalence are generated by the continuous and multiple variety of distracting images in the conscious mind. They land in there because of the lack of ability to *choose* a definitive purpose. Nature abhors a vacuum and it will fill your mind with something, if you don't consciously choose something. The "not choosing" causes us to stall or put off things we'd really like to do, sometimes for a very long time. This is when something I call the "Magpie Effect" kicks in. As entrepreneurs there are a lot of things you either have to learn or delegate to others to move ahead. So how do you choose from the seemingly unlimited amount of options that can help you move forward? Choose the outcome *first*. Anything less is to leave yourself wide open to the magpie. He will fill your mind with lots of bright shiny solutions to your challenges, all which have varying amounts of value and usefulness, but on their own without an end purpose they just become some extra stuff which you've learnt about but still haven't implemented.

I absolutely love simplicity. Make it hard to understand and I'm not interested. I've realised over the years that there is an awful lot of truth in the idea that any fool can make something sound complicated, but it's hard to make it simple. It takes real skill to explain complicated ideas so that you can communicate them to others properly. One of my mentors once explained to me that "You do not understand something until you can explain it to someone else so that *they* understand it." So let's keep it simple.

 One of the biggest handicaps to a person's success is the ability to get things done. Remember, it isn't how much you know that the world rewards and remembers it's what you get done. We don't want to work harder, we want to work more effectively.

Sir Walter Raleigh who built the great tobacco empire was asked how he accomplished so much in such a short time. Raleigh replied, "When there is anything to do, I start it." Most people's productivity resembles the movements of a jar of chutney sitting in the back of a dark kitchen cupboard. It's not a lack of ability that keeps them going so slow, it's a lack of focus.

Because I like simplicity, over the years I have broken down productivity into six simple steps that takes five minutes to complete. It's all very logical and you will understand it completely.

However, what you need is the pig headed discipline to spend five minutes getting into the habit of doing it daily. If you do, the pay-off will be huge I promise. Not just in productivity, but in your own energy, fulfilment and excitement.

Let's get into it. "I haven't got the time" is probably the most common excuse we can make in business, and the reason why it's so popular is that it gently fobs off people (who are asleep) and kind of gives you a half-decent excuse. In our country being "busy" is virtuous. I haven't got the time, is really born out of lack of definite purpose, which causes lack of priority, which causes indecision. If your purpose were to fly to Barcelona tomorrow, you would have a definitive order of priorities that you would decide upon in order to get there. No purpose, no order. In my experience most people in business don't take the time to plan and take action because all of their time is consumed by reacting to the business they have already built. The focus is mainly on getting through, rather than getting on with a purpose.

Get Proactive!

As I mentioned at the start of the book, at age 28, I bought the franchise for a global tool manufacturer and was lucky to partner with the UK's number one Sales manager, Andy Walker. Andy was not just my manager but Mentor and trainer. He was constantly reminding me of the need to be proactive rather than reactive in business and this was evident in everything he did. Every meeting we had was highly productive and to the point. Because his time was shared out amongst the other salespeople I soon learned that I had to have a strict agenda in order to get the help I needed quickly. Work-time was for working. Socialising was left for after-hours in the pub. What I did was break down the various areas of sales in to my "impact areas." An impact area is any part of your company that has a direct impact on your bottom line profits. These could be sales, marketing, product creation, customer relations or accounting for example. In order to improve these areas you need to give them a dedicated hour a week of focused time when everyone involved can improve in that area. Top of the priorities list was sales development, because this is the highest income-generating activity there is.

Six Steps To Getting Things Done

Step 1: Touch Once

Tell me if this sounds familiar. You come into your office and on your desk are a couple of letters, various documents, books and folders. You look at the letter, read a bit of it and decide that you'll get around to it when your less busy. Quick check on Facebook or Linked-In to see if anyone has responded to your posts. Phone rings and you get pulled in another direction for 10-15 minutes. Then you get back to starting the day and "ping," an email lands, so you decide to open it up and see what it is. The email needs responding to but you will *do it later* because there are other things you need to do first. If you spend an hour per day, scattered throughout the day, revisiting or re-reading documents or emails you waste *six weeks* per year where no action is taken. The rule is, if you touch it, take action on it. Don't open that email until you are ready to deal with it. Email is probably the biggest time suck in your productive working week. Two great keys to email management is to:

1. Use very descriptive email subject lines.

2. Block out time to respond.

Say you send an email that has the subject header of "Simon Gilbert Seminar" and your friend writes back something that looks like this:

To: Lucy

From: Claire

Subject : Simon Gilbert Seminar

Yes, I booked it last night after the webinar. By the way did you talk to Richard about the production costs and whether we can go ahead?

The email goes back and forth about the production costs with Richard, but it still has "Simon Gilbert Seminar" in the subject line. A week later someone asks about the production costs with Richard. One of the eight emails has the information, but you have to open all eight in order to find what you need. Email can be the death of productivity and keep you in the reactive mode all day long.

Get into the habit of deciding when you will look at and consequently respond to your emails. What works for me are first thing early in the morning , say 7am, after dinner at 1pm and then 6pm at night. If your computer signals when you have an email, turn the alert off. Email is there for your convenience.

Concentration is like a muscle and it strengthens as you concentrate more for longer periods. If you stop concentrating every time you get distracted by something like your mobile or email, you lessen your ability to concentrate and become less effective in any situation that requires concentration. As ever, as you go through these six things don't think about whether you've heard them before, just ask, am I doing them?

> *"To know and not to do is not to know at all..."*
> *– Bruce Lee*

Step 2: Super Six List

My next suggestion for you and this really is the absolute key to productivity is the **Super Six List.** It's been said before, and I agree, that keeping a list will double your productivity right away.

In the early 1900s, Charles Schwab was President of the Bethlehem Steel Company, a small steel company that was struggling. A business consultant named Ivy Lee told Schwab that he could share in 15 minutes a strategy with Schwab's managers that would double productivity at least. When Schwab inquired about the price for the help, Lee said, "After using it for six months, you can pay me whatever you think its worth."

Ivy Lee, shared with Schwab his secret of writing a list of things he needed to do each day. He told Schwab to write on an index card the six most important things he must do the next day in order of importance. "Tomorrow morning start on number one, and stay with it until you have completed it. Then go on to number two and then number three and then number four… Don't worry if you don't complete everything by the end of the day. At least you will have completed the most important tasks. Do this every day." said Lee.

"Try it out as long as you wish and then send me a cheque for what YOU think it's worth."

The whole meeting lasted about twenty-five minutes. Two weeks later, Schwab sent Lee a cheque for £16,000!

£16,000 in 1910 would today be worth over £175,000 today.

Did it work? Well, in five years it turned the unknown Bethlehem Steel Company into the biggest independent steel producer in the world; made Schwab a hundred million dollar fortune, and the best known steel man alive at that time. Another reason as to why it works so well is because if you write your list the night before, the subconscious treats the entire list as a cybernetic goal and goes to work on that list whilst your sleeping, in order to come up with ideas and solutions to the most efficient way of completing it. It's like having the most efficient computer in the world working on your list whilst you get some sleep. Why wouldn't you use it?

If you can go through each day taking the highest priority actions, it doesn't matter if some of the things don't get done because you will have been working on the most important tasks-it's just so simple.

So get going today - start using Ivy Lee's **Super Six** system.

Step 3: Plan Time Allocation

If one or more items on your list is too big to accomplish in one day and there are other stuff that does need to get done, then simply write down the amount of time you will allocate to the prioritised list in one day. For example, my first book *"How Big is Your But!"* took me 18 months to write because I had no plan and no system. I was scattered in my approach and wasn't focused. My next book took me just 20 days to thrash out the content because I allocated time and focus to the project. I figured a 200 page book could be split up into 20 days x 10 pages a day. And I had a system. Interestingly enough, because that is what I wanted that is what I got. What have you been putting off for years? Or what important strategies are you just not getting to because they might take too much time? Just break things down into small chunks of time, and get on with it!

Parkinson's Law

It is a commonplace observation that work expands to fill the time available for its completion. This is known as *Parkinson's Law*. Thus, an elderly lady of leisure could spend the entire day in writing and posting a postcard to her grandson in Harrogate. An hour could be spent in finding the postcard, another in hunting for spectacles, half-an-hour in a search for the address, an hour and a quarter in writing the damn thing and twenty minutes in deciding whether or not to walk to the pillar-box in the next street or take the Honda Civic. The total effort which would occupy a busy man would be nine minutes all told. Good enough and DONE is better than perfect and never done!

My typical day list might look like:

1. Work on new book-1 hour.

2. Client meeting-2 hours

3. Work on marketing plan-0.5 hours

4. Plan FEAR DVD series-1 hour

5. Group Skype Call-0.5 hours

6. Work on Client proposal-1 hour

Add up the total amount of hours for your productive tasks. Here it comes to six hours. A good guide to go by is your six most important things should take around six hours, but it obviously depends on the value and importance of each task.

Step 4: Plan the Day

Start with a Clear Desk

Clear your desk the night before in order that you start clean in the morning. There is good reason for this. Information you receive from your peripheral vision, that's the side of your eyes, impacts you subliminally and has more emotional content. If you have ever seen a film at the cinema and then watched that same film on your TV at home, you know it doesn't have the same emotional impact.

Why? Well, excluding the Dolby surround sound you may have, you are seeing everything in your central vision on your TV, whereas on the cinema screen you are picking things up out of the corner of your eyes and that has more emotional impact. In the same way if you leave books, files and letters on the side of your desk, it's almost like they can speak, saying things like, *"Don't forget me!, I'm still here you know"*....which of course breaks concentration and focus.

With Imagination Time

Allow for time to meditate on your goals, plans, or even something that your stuck on. Allocate a couple of hours during the week for this imagination time. Doing this could easily fool you into thinking this is a real waste of time, but it really isn't. If you do it habitually you will find it's the time when you will get superconscious solutions to your current problems.

You will begin to get hooked on the idea of this imagination time when you start to see just how fast and how simple it works. A simple way to carry out this exercise is to write a focused question at the top of a clear sheet of paper and allow your mind to come up with the answers. For example: "How can we *possibly* increase sales by 40% in the next 6 months?" Just allow the ideas to flow. The rule is long term thinking improves short term decision making.

Allow for "Could You Just?"

No one is naïve enough to think that you are not going to get interrupted from time to time. This could come in the form of customer enquires or staff interruptions or deliveries. Plan into your day 2 half-hour blocks of time that allow for these *"could you just"* miscellaneous meetings. These are the things that you have to react to that will throw you off schedule.

If you have planned at least two half-hour slots of reactive time, when you get back to it you've actually built in buffers, so you get back on schedule as planned.

Identify Your 80/20

We've heard it a hundred times: 20 percent of your efforts brings in 80 percent of your results. As I've mentioned before it's like a badge of honour to say you are busy. Well, so what? Busy doing stuff that are high-results producing activities or low value tasks?

Many people stress themselves out with hundreds of low value tasks so they can justify "Being Busy" but when you look at their actual productivity, it's very low. The truth is out of the thousands of things your mind can "Magpie" you with, only 3-4 matter right now in the moment.

The 80/20 also means that 20 percent of your customers accounts for 80 percent of your sales, 20 percent of your products or services will account for 80 percent of your profits and most important in this section of the book it means 20 percent of your list will account for 80% of the value in the list.

The sad fact is that most people will procrastinate on the most valuable and important things whilst attending to the things that contribute very little to results. Instantly identifying your 80/20's gives you clarity on what needs to be done, and identifies those things that could be delegated, outsourced or just plain dropped altogether.

Step 5: Dump It!

Studies have shown in the UK that 82 percent of all filed or stored information is *never* referred to again. Working in conjunction with the touch it once strategy, I use the Three D's principle to decide to either,

✓ Do it,

✓ Delegate it, or

✓ Dump it!

To determine whether or not to keep something, ask yourself, "Will it really hurt me to dump this in the bin or shredder?" Could you get it back if you really needed it? Using this system, only on very rare occasions do I wish I had held onto something. In comparison to the distracting and debilitating effects of "mind clutter" it is easily worth the price to pay.

Step 6: Start Right Now!

If you don't act on an idea that could really help you straight away it's unlikely you ever act on it at all. One of the keys to success is to just start something immediately when you hear or see a great idea that would help you towards your goals.

As we go through our days, so many times our mind will wander off to the things we wish we had in our lives – Most of the time we quickly file those away in a "someday" folder, or jot them down on a bucket list we insist on keeping. Someday Island is where dreams go on holiday and never come back......

What if you made a decision right now to make your life so FULL, so COMPLETE and so EXHILERATING that you didn't need a bucket list, and the thought of "someday" could never trump present day?

Now the main question – ***Why not do that?***

This is your life. Every precious moment is fading into the next – the past is gaining weight, while the future is slipping away, and the present is hardly being appreciated or capitalised on.

It's NOW. That's the only time you and I ever have. The world is smaller than ever and moving at an ever-increasing speed of FAST FORWARD.

Overwhelm and procrastination have quickly become a part of our global paradigm. In order to stop the cycle and create the lifestyle you've been dreaming of – a decision needs to be made and work needs to be done-right now. If you are one of those who make up their minds today and change them again tomorrow, you are doomed to failure. If you are not sure of the best course of action, it's much better to shut your eyes and move in the dark than to remain still and make no move at all. You can do it-I know you can. So get on with it! You've got everything it takes to be a winner, so get rid of the idea that you can't.

Within the pages of this book, I've talked about the actions, thoughts and beliefs possessed by successful people. And I'm sure that, by now, you understand why having a rich life is not just about the money; it's about how you think and what you create with those thoughts.

Now it's time for you to implement these techniques into your own life. For change to happen more rapidly for you, you know you must DECIDE on your goal, alter the programming in your subconscious mind so it aligns with this goal and BELIEVE you will get it. By practicing and building upon the ideas I've presented here, you will be well on your way to living a new and exciting life...

Eliminate all the beliefs standing in your way and you can literally achieve anything you really want to. Everything starts in the mind first, so remember, have fun and ***THINK SMART - LIVE RICH!***

Simon is also the author of the book, **"How Big Is Your But!"** which is available through his website or on Amazon.co.uk. Simon may be available for a small number of speaking engagements each year with his keynote presentation, **"How to Release the Mental Handbrake Sabotaging Your Success in Business"**, specifically for the Sales, Entrepreneurial and Network Marketing Industries.

Email: simon@simonjgilbert.com for more details.

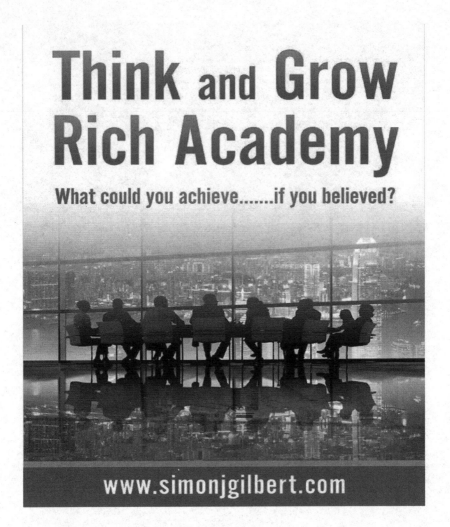

If you'd like to accelerate your results fast and be considered as a participant in your local **TAGR Academy™** Mastermind please go to **www.simonjgilbert.com** and fill out the application form you'll find there. If you'd like to be considered as a 121 client and permanently eliminate ANY belief holding you back or get trained as a consultant to deliver the **SHIFT B.E.L.I.E.F.S System™** you'll also find the details there too.